The *Caurāsī Pad* of Śrī Hit Harivaṁś

Asian Studies at Hawaii, No. 16

The *Caurāsī Pad* of Śrī Hit Harivaṁś

Introduction, Translation, Notes, and edited Braj Bhāṣā text

Charles S. J. White

ASIAN STUDIES PROGRAM
UNIVERSITY OF HAWAII
THE UNIVERSITY PRESS OF HAWAII

Manufactured in the United States of America

Library of Congress Cataloging in Publication Data

Hita Harivamsa Gosvami, 1502–1552.
The Caurasi pad of Sri Hit Harivams.

(Asian studies at Hawaii; no. 16)
Includes bibliographical references.
1. Krishna—Poetry. 2. Rādhā (Hindu deity)—Poetry. I. White, Charles S. J., 1929- II. Title. III. Series.
DS3.A2A82 no. 16 [PK1967.9.H56] 891'.43'12 76-54207
ISBN 0-8248-0359-0

TO MY TEACHERS

Contents

Preface	ix
Introduction	3
Part I. The Background	3
The Early Context	3
Primary Literature	14
Literary Conventions	16
The Historical Question	19
Part II. Toward Interpretation of the *Caurāsī Pad* of Śrī Hit Harivaṁś	22
The Founder of the Rādhāvallabha Sampradāy	26
Teachings of the Rādhāvallabha Sampradāy	28
The Cult of Rādhāvallabha	31
Hindi Literature	34
The Literary Works of Śrī Hit Harivaṁś	35
The Letters	36
Sanskrit Works	36
Hindi Works	37
Poetic Style in the *Caurāsī Pad*	39
The Translation	55
The *Braj Bhāṣā* Text of the *Caurāsī Pad*	119

Preface

The *Caurāsī Pad, The Eighty-four Stanzas,* describes the union of the supreme deities of the universe—Rādhā and Kṛṣṇa—manifestations of a high god, Viṣṇu. These beings fell in love at a timeless moment and their love play will endure forever. The action of the poem takes place under the guise of human life in a countryside setting of northern India; the tone, apart from its religious use, is lyrical rather than solemn. Although these divinities cannot, strictly speaking, be likened to the lovers in a popular romance, Rādhā and Kṛṣṇa are nevertheless the most popular lovers in the Hindu religion. Their idealized physical forms and personalities express a final truth that love is the very ground of reality and that man's destiny is to contemplate that love with consummate rapture. Love owes its importance to its source, Rādhā, the supreme principle, a goddess through whom Kṛṣṇa experiences the ecstasy of eternal union. Bliss, being, and life flow from her. Sexuality thus seems to have an inherently holy value for the gods. For man it may become the image of the most sacred, transcendent experience or knowledge.

From the beginning of the present era Indians have studied the qualities of sexual life to a rare degree and have carried out their investigations in the spirit of science. Sanskrit imaginative literature, however, was also uncommonly aware of the character of human emotions and the extent to which man is absorbed in love, *śṛṇgāra* or *madhura*. The Hindu, perhaps of all the great cultures of the world, has been most typically "erotic" in its historical style (including the voluptuous character of many of its artistic expressions) but with the intense refinement that is present in all aspects of its life.

This may puzzle those who view India as the land of the ascetic for whom the world is a lure and to whom sexual life is anathema. Quite simply, in Indian culture the two emphases coexist. Ascetics in the ideal sense are few in India, but they exercise a deep influence upon the masses whom they lead in religious affairs. These rare men and women seem to extend the continuum of human possibilities and do not necessarily demand of others such rigors as they demand of themselves. But the strong ideal of asceticism could and did impose itself in a symbolic way upon a wide variety of activities and ultimately created a *yoga* of eros, the *tantra,* with its disciples. Besides the indigenous influences, the development of a sensibility in this regard in the *bhakti* sects is probably related to the religious synthesis that medieval Hinduism achieved under the influence of Islām, and especially under its mystic specialists, the Sūfīs, whose teaching includes erotic symbolism to assist the soul in its ascent toward Allah.

The thirty or forty miles from Āgrā to Vṛndāvan lead from the early Mogul capital, the home of the Tāj Mahal, to a small city that mythically antedates the Muslim settlement of northern India. In fact, Vṛndāvan received its impetus to become a religious center from the effect of the Muslim conquest upon Hinduism. The subservient position in which the Hindus then found themselves stimulated further development of the *bhakti* or devotional cult, which emphasized emotionalism and a sense of dependence upon a benign savior who promised an unending happiness in paradise in return for faith during life.

There is a world of contrast between Āgrā and Vṛndāvan, especially when one considers their present status and their circumstances in the sixteenth and seventeenth centuries. Historically Āgrā and its environs were adorned with masterpieces of north Indian Muslim art and crowned with the Tāj Mahal itself; Vṛndāvan was a patch of jungle that developed into a religious center but without apparent reliance upon architectural grandeur and finesse.[1] The old Āgrā, the frontier town at the edge of the Rajasthān desert, grew to be a famous capital, though its situation was always precarious. The Āgrā of today, ostensibly a Hindu city, adorns its religious preference in muted colors amid the Mogul architecture. One sees the contrast—the seclusion of the Hindu *bhakti* renaissance alongside its tomb-building masters. Once one turns from the Delhi-Āgrā complex and leaves behind the historical mortuary grandeur, one still finds among the people a Hinduism as lively today as it must have been in the sixteenth and seventeenth centuries. It was to the astonishment of succeeding generations that works of literature of extraordinary brilliance emerged from those humble byways, those lanes and alleys weaving behind the imposing display of the dominant culture. In their own way these literary monuments rise to the glory of the Hindu religious faith that produced them and rival the splendid architectural expressions of the Muslim rulers.

Entering Mathurā brings one within the sacred precincts—and near Vṛndāvan—where Rādhā and Kṛṣṇa were united for the salvation of mankind in the moonlit forest along the banks of the Jamunā. F. S. Growse, a British civil administrator who recorded a history of the district, notes the words of another writer, Tod:

> Though the groves of Brinda in which Krishna disported with the Gopis no longer resound to the echoes of his flute; though the waters of the Jamuna are daily polluted with the blood of the sacred kine; still it is the holy land of the pilgrim, the sacred Jordan of his fancy, on whose banks he may sit and weep, as did the banished Israelite of old, for the glories of Mathurā, his Jerusalem.[2]

The reader may well envision such a sacred land, peopled with divine beings and their associates, symbolic of the relationship between God and man, as he tries to perceive the Hinduism of the *Braj* land in the Middle Ages, and in particular of the sect devoted to Rādhā, the Rādhāvallabha Sampradāy. The exposition of the ideals of this sect through a work of literature is the main concern of this monograph.

I feel very privileged to have been able to visit the setting and to undertake the translation of the *Śrī Hit Caurāsī Pad,* or simply *Caurāsī Pad,* of Śrī Hit Harivaṁś. There is in the realm of literature in India enormous opportunity for little-known works to be read, translated, and interpreted in an appropriate context. The value of such studies should be at least as much for their contribution to our pleasure in man expressing himself through his art as for the clarification of some part of the enigma of a foreign nation in its cultural and religious distinctiveness.

The following work could scarcely have been completed without the cooperation of members of the Rādhāvallabha Sampradāy, the sect founded by Śrī Hit Harivaṁś, who interpreted certain of the difficult passages in the text through references to the sect's private commentarial works. I am especially indebted to Śrī Hit Jīvan Gosvāmī, a descendant of the founder of the sect, who helped me deal with abstruse passages in the text and problems in the context of the *Caurāsī Pad,* and who guided me through the sacred places of the Sampradāy.

The translation itself is meant to be as nearly literal as sense and syntax in normal English would allow; at the same time I have made no effort to recapitulate the rhyming and rhythmic effects of the original *Braj Bhāṣā* (Hindi) with the complexities of the *pad.* Whatever poetry the reader experiences will depend upon how successfully the translator has transcreated the original stanza form and its meaning into free verse. The attempt has been made in transliteration to be consistent according to standard methods for Indian languages. The reader will find both Sanskrit and Hindi spellings, depending on the setting of the discussion. Where possible, technical terms of a religious, philosophical, or literary nature are given in their Sanskrit forms. Certain place names with well-known English equivalents, such as Delhi, appear in the text.

I wish I had been able to thank F. E. Keay,[3] F. S. Growse, and others who suggested in their earlier writings the excellence of the poetry of the *Caurāsī Pad,* and thus led me to a type of translation that was very enjoyable. The statements of their enthusiastic discovery of the literature and religious life of medieval India have not been surpassed.

I am deeply indebted to the late Director of the Hindi Institute of Āgrā University, Dr. M. P. Gupta, who made available every facility at his disposal to assist my research. He regularly set aside time in the midst of his own full program of study to give advice to his foreign students. In particular, he helped me find an able research assistant, Mr. H. N. Yadau, a fellow of the Hindi Institute of Āgrā University. Mr. Yadau consulted on the translation of the text and served as my adviser during visits to Vṛndāvan. I would like to thank Dr. Swatantra K. Pidara, a Fellow in the Oriental Studies Department of the University of Pennsylvania and my former student, for his editorial assistance, and Mrs. Seetha Neelakanthan, librarian of the Adyar Research Library of the Theosophical Society, Adyar, Madras, for her guidance and proofreading. Professor Charlotte Vaudeville of the Sorbonne, with whom I studied *Braj Bhāṣā* and with whom I have enjoyed many inspiring discussions of Indian religion and literature, is the model for all Western scholars of medieval Hindi poetry. I am grateful to the officers and members of the American Institute of Indian Studies for the fellowship that enabled me to undertake the research in connection with this study and to Dr. D. D. Karvé and the staff of the American Institute of Indian Studies in Poona for the courtesies that were extended throughout my association with them. Mrs. Gladys Smith graciously assisted with typing. I would like to thank Professor Edmund Robins of *The Mexico Quarterly Review* and The University of the Americas, Puebla, Mexico—with whom I studied the writing of poetry long before setting out to learn about Indian religion—for first publishing stanzas five, sixteen, twenty, and twenty-seven in his journal. I would like to offer a final word of appreciation to Professor N. Sundaram of the Department of Hindi, Presidency College, Madras, with whom I consulted on matters pertaining to Hindi prosody and who hand-lettered the Hindi text published in this book.

Charles S. J. White
The American University

NOTES

1. There are, however, photographs of ruined temples in F. S. Growse's *Mathura: A District Memoir,* revised and abridged (North-Western Provinces and Oudh Government Press, 1883), and I have seem some examples. There is evidence of great skill in carving but otherwise the buildings were constructed on a rather limited architectural scale.
2. Growse, op. cit., title page.
3. F. W. Keay, *A History of Hindī Literature* (Calcutta: Oxford University Press, 1920).

The *Caurāsī Pad* of Śrī Hit Harivaṁś

Introduction

Part I. The Background

The cult of Rādhā appears at the end of a long history of Hindu religious development to which every aspect of the Hinduism preceding it may have made some contribution. I shall try to develop some part of that historical context from which the *Caurāsī Pad,* the celebration of the love of Rādhā and Kṛṣṇa, emerged.

The Early Context

The term *bhakti*[1] derives from a Sanskrit root *bhaj*. Among its various meanings, *bhaj* implies the division or distribution of goods and the giving of gifts as well as the honoring, loving, and adoring of someone, usually a divinity. In its accepted current usage, *bhakti* refers to a spectrum of religious practices as well as to the lives of saints and to literary expressions that have been inspired by a feeling of personal devotion to a god.

A dominant motif in *bhakti* is the desire for an experience of union or association with God, a kind of transcendental delight. Sanskrit supplies the term *rasa,* the savor of a thing, even the flavor of a delicious food or drink. In poetry it refers to the appropriate emotion arising from the special arrangements of excellent language.[2] In religion, *rasa* is that bliss, or grace, that spreads through every mundane event, impregnating it with the very essence of God. In human terms the *rasika,* one adept in *rasa,* enjoys more fully because he is able to savor the quality of a particular thing. For a devotee of God such savoring runs throughout life, in the manner prescribed by the central experiences of his unique approach to God. Thus the *rasa* of Rāma is considered different from that of Kṛṣṇa. As we shall see later on, the *rasa* that surges from devotion to Rādhā can give the devotee the sense that ecstasy flows through all the known and unknown worlds; the devotee regards himself as a point in an ocean of bliss.

By contrast with the personal devotion of *bhakti,* from early in Indian history there were religious specialists, such as the priests of the Brāhmaṇa literature, who desired to have as much power as the gods—indeed to take the place of the gods. In its first phase this quest for power led to the transformation of the Vedic sacrifice from a ceremony of supplication and propitiation to a magical attempt to bring the power of the gods under the control of the worshipper. This trend toward ritualism was complemented by an esoteric tradition, deriving perhaps from the so-called Śramaṇas. It ultimately gave rise to the Jain and Buddhist monastic orders, and to certain philosophical developments that taught the essential divinity of man and/or a oneness with the divine. By moving in this direction the sense of the divine reality became more and more internalized and subjective.

Indeed, one must assert the hypothesis that the tension between the subjective, monistic tendency and an objective, dualistic tendency remained a source of creativity in Hinduism. The monistic, with its emphasis upon the oneness of all spirit in the universe, has had exclusive appeal for a minority of thinkers and mystics who considered that logically, or as the result of spiritual experience, oneness was a more adequate way to describe the cosmic reality than to speak in terms of duality. In spite of the considerable impact of monistic thinking, the apparent dualism of the phenomenal in relation to the spiritual and of the soul in relation to God also had numerous supporters. These contrasting positions developed through the earliest Hindu attempts to state a consistent philosophical position.

In the Upaniṣads, the last section of the Veda, insights into the cosmic law, the moral law, and the nature of a spiritual absolute, *Brahman,* began to take shape. As the earlier yearning for power over the cosmos became spiritualized, the essential sameness of the self and the cosmic order was advocated. The spirit of this monistic thinking inspires many passages in the Upaniṣads; for example: "Verily, this whole world is Brahman: Tranquil, let one worship It as that from which he came forth, as that into which he will be dissolved, as that in which he breathes" (*Chāndogya Upaniṣad* III. 14. 1); "Verily, what is called Brahman—that is the same as what the space within a person is. Verily, what the space within a person is—that is the same as what the space here within the heart is" (*Chānd.* III. 12. 7); "This Self, verily, is a world of all created beings" (*Bṛhadāraṇyaka Upaniṣad* I. 4. 16).[3]

However, it requires a more refined philosophical statement to encompass the relationship between what exists phenomenologically in its variety and mutability and the essentially unchanging, ontological source that was imagined for existence. Thus the esoteric nature of the internal experience of divine reality is increasingly emphasized. "Him who is hard to see, entered into the hidden, set in the secret place, dwelling in the depth, primeval" *(Kaṭha Upaniṣad* II. 12; *Śvetāśvatara Upaniṣad VI. 2);* and "Though he is hidden in all things, that Soul (Ātman) shines not forth. But He is seen by subtle seers with superior, subtle intellect" (*Kaṭha* III. 12; *Śvet.* IV. 15).[4] Further development led to the objective tendency—the distinguishing of the individual soul from *Brahman* in certain passages so that there might be a relationship between them.

> . . . the religious world view of the author of the Śvetāśvatara leads to the doctrine that the Supreme Being is related to the individual soul not only as the Perfect and adorable Lord who exists within the individual without destroying its individuality on the one hand, or His own essential greatness on the other, but also as the "Kindly One" who shows grace to the finite individual. (*Śvet.* I. 6; III. 20)[5]

The teachings of the Upaniṣads do not appear in well-organized systems as set forth in later Indian philosophy. They are partly discursive and partly metaphoric, and they gather and blend the leading spiritual teachings found in the earlier Vedic writings with the personal commentary of a teacher. In part they are summaries or anthologies in a narrative setting and, as such, they merit the title given to them in India of Vedānta, the summing-up of the Veda. Even after the Upaniṣadic period it was customary for Indian metaphysical systems to refer to the Vedānta as the basis of orthodoxy. However, the teachings of the Vedānta allow for a wide latitude in interpretation. It was thus possible for opposing philosophies—Advaita or monism, and Viśiṣṭādvaita or dualism—to be based on different Upaniṣadic texts, or at times on the same texts. Systems of thought began to arise advocating either a monistic or a dualistic understanding of the Absolute, God, the soul or spiritual entity in man, and the apparently nonsentient physical universe. The dualist philosophies tended to support devotion to a personal God although monist thought sometimes made a contribution to this end.[6]

To understand the increasing importance of the dualist position as the classical period advanced we must examine a chain of circumstances leading to the development of exalted theism. First is the issue of the way in which the "savior deity" Viṣṇu emerges as a dominating factor in Indian life. The name derives from a root *viṣ,* meaning to pervade. We know that devotion to Viṣṇu begins in the Vedic religion. (Vedic religion refers to those developments prior to the end of the Upaniṣadic period, circa 600 B.C.E. Hinduism, properly speaking, commences after that date.) Moreover, "we may even surmise his ascendancy to have constituted, if not a 'reaction' of proto-Hinduism to the religion of the Nordic invaders [the Aryans who allegedly entered India near the beginning of the second millennium B.C.E.], then a coming to the surface of the beliefs of those masses whose voice is but imperfectly heard in the Ṛgveda."[7] It is a complex problem to delimit the religious contribution of the various elements within Indian religion at this early period, but several general themes contribute to the system of ideas about Viṣṇu.

First of all, Viṣṇu has affinities for the symbolisms and realities of fertility, and therefore is a divinity of vegetation as well as of seawaters, where he lies as upon a bed.[8] He is called Madhu and Madhava, the names of the two months of the spring season; through his avatar, Kṛṣṇa, he is the father of Kāma, the god of love; he is both the protector of women in childbirth and the guarantor of human fertility as well as being, at times, the symbolic summation of sexual potentiality when he is thought to be androgynous.[9] In short, Viṣṇu displayed part of his character in reference to the needs of man for a fertile earth to produce food, as well as man's need for his own fertility and the continuance of the human species.

A second series of ideas, arising in part from the first, has to do with Viṣṇu's benevolence. He is represented in the *Atharvaveda* (7. 26. 8) as the divinity to whom to appeal for riches: "From the sky, O Viṣṇu, or also from the earth, from the great wide atmosphere, O Viṣṇu, fill thy hands abundantly with good things; and bestow them from the right and from the left."[10] Moreover, some of Viṣṇu's names—Vasu, Vasuda, Vasuprada—refer to wealth or possessions, *vasu;* perhaps he is the divinity of cattle, Gopati, Govidāṃ Patiḥ, "the Lord of the cattle," because, in addition to being objects of piety, cows are wealth.[11] His beneficence is raised to grandeur in his aspect as a solar divinity. Here he shares with Indra the triumph in the cosmic battle with Vṛtra, the dragon, who holds back the waters necessary for the fertility of the earth. Viṣṇu by epic times has usurped Indra's role as fighter for the gods and has acquired the epithet Atīndra—"He who is over Indra." He is that divinity, as well, who maintains the cosmic order by propping up the sky and striding, *Viṣṇukramāḥ,* from the earth to the heavenly places.[12] His three strides provide a kinetic image of the pervasiveness of the deity throughout the worlds, the universe, and space. The visual coordinate of the strides is the sight of the ascent of the sun from the horizon through the upper atmosphere to the zenith of heaven. The rising of Viṣṇu is a part of the drama of cosmic confrontation between Viṣṇu and Indra on the one side and Vṛtra on the other; the energy or power necessary for man's salvation is released into the world as a result of Viṣṇu's striding. The light of heaven becomes man's salvation so that we have a mode of understanding Viṣṇu that will be developed in the later, more complete image of the deity as savior.

A third theme, symbolic and sacrificial in character, extends Viṣṇu's capacities in various directions. In the Brāhmaṇas it is recorded that "Viṣṇu is not only constantly declared to be the sacrifice . . . he is also the protector of the oblations . . . besides, the sacrificer is identified with him . . . . "[13] Prajāpati, the great creator god of the Brahmaṇas, is linked with Viṣṇu in the sacrifice, and in the theriomorphic incarnations as boar and tortoise that are later important in Viṣṇu's myth. All of the elements of the sacrifice come to be identified with the evolving character of Viṣṇu. The one who makes the sacrifice is imitating the deeds of Viṣṇu. It is obvious that this central rite of the Vedic religion, with its continuing importance for the priestly caste, had the capacity to reveal new meanings to the developing religious insight. The offering of Prajāpati or Viṣṇu in the sacrifice became identified with all of the supposedly beneficial effects of the rite for maintaining the cosmic order and redounding upon the sacrificer in the form of vital powers—the control of fertility and productivity. When the sacrifice itself had ceased to hold the attention of the whole religious community, it had nevertheless left as its heir a living sacrifice in the form of Viṣṇu. His universal character is revealed in the *yūpa,* the sacrificial post—which was both the phallus, indicating the fertilizing power flowing from heaven into the earth, and the cosmic tree or pillar, the channel along which communication ascends and descends between the celestial and terrestrial worlds. The cosmic tree pervades the universe and seems essential to the maintenance of the cosmic structure. Thus the *yūpa* signifies the primordial character of the relationship between Viṣṇu and the various aspects of his interaction with the earth and its special concerns, and with the larger sphere of cosmic activity of which he was the mystic center. In a similar fashion the navel, or omphalos, of Viṣṇu becomes the source from which arises, traditionally, the lotus. There rests the newborn Brahmā, in this case the sustaining principle of the world, or the universe itself. Like the cosmic pillar, the navel is a focal point for the creative activity of the god, and especially his powers of fertility. By virtue of being the center, the omphalos calls to mind the origin of the universal power that sustains or creates the universe as a whole.

Through the labyrinth of Indian religion the paths of Viṣṇu cross those of other deities at every turn and every level. An encounter with Viṣṇu was often final for a less vital image of the deity, or it could mean that Viṣṇu took him into the company of his many faithful followers who had discovered themselves to be aspects of their master. However, Viṣṇu was not content, so to speak, to be monolithically One. Therefore, he produced avatars (Sanskrit *avatāra,* a "descent" of Viṣṇu) and dramatically provided the material for the development of many of the schools and cults of *bhakti*. In the *Mahābhārata* the ten traditional avatars of Viṣṇu are mentioned as follows: the fish, Matsya; the tortoise, Kūrma; the boar, Varāha; the man-lion, Nṛsiṁha; the dwarf, Vāmana; Paraśurāma; Rāmacandra; Kṛṣṇa; Buddha; Kalkī. Of these, Rāmacandra and Kṛṣṇa are outstanding, but the other avatars, human and animal, have their roles in the salvation of the world or of the devotees. In later times the number of recognized incarnations grew to twenty-five or more and included such historical persons as Śrī Vallabhācarya and Śrī Caitanya.

The circumstances in which a god finds it necessary to change his form either through metamorphosis or incarnation are found in other religions besides Hinduism, for example, the animal epiphanies of the Greek gods. In the earlier Vedic period Indra had been characterized by his morphological versatility and, as in so many other ways, his influence upon Viṣṇu is evident. Viṣṇu's animal and human avatars were not simply demonstrations of divine power:

> In the animal manifestations the well-known motive of the animal aiding or assisting man was given a more universal and elevated application. In general the Viṣṇuite avatars have essentially diverged from the primitive motif of a god descending to the earth. The god is born each time for a specific purpose. When the dharma is not followed, Viṣṇu appears on earth in one of his avatars for the rescue of the good, for the preservation of the world and its culture, for the destruction of the evil doers and the establishment of dharma.[14]

Representations of Viṣṇu are numerous, and the variety in the placement of his attributes makes the analysis of his different iconic forms a complex study. Generally speaking, it is Viṣṇu's universal and benevolent character which prevails in the art that depicts him. Prior to his "appearance" he is pervasive throughout the universe as structure and hence personally unmanifested. As the principle of power and being in the cosmic ocean he "appears" as Nārāyaṇa, who sleeps on the back of the water serpent Ananta. This is his most mysterious iconic description. He is usually depicted as a handsome young man with blue skin, standing in a graceful posture and holding symbolic objects in each of his four hands: a discus, a club, a conch shell, and a lotus. The arrangement of these objects signifies exactly which aspect of Viṣṇu is being shown. In his historical incarnations, he assumes many more complex guises, depending on the exigencies of different myths.[15]

In the classical period when the "power" of the various important gods became personified in goddesses, Lakṣmī is identified as Viṣṇu's consort, although in Vedic times she had had different associations. Her name implies wealth and fortune, but she is known also as Śrī, the goddess of beauty. As Lakṣmī, Viṣṇu's feminine aspect maintains an independent existence and has always been honored by most Hindus as the patroness of wealth and all manner of success. Through the development of the cult of avatars Lakṣmī follows Viṣṇu into incarnation: namely, for Rāma as Sītā, for Vāmana as Kamalā, and so on. Hence, when Rukmaṇī, a partner for Kṛṣṇa, appears in an earlier age, the stage is prepared for the later advent of Rādhā. We will discuss this aspect of the Vaiṣṇava cult at greater length in the second part of the Introduction. It is sufficient to note here that the concept of a goddess consort emerges together with Viṣṇu from the complex topography for the masculine deity.

From the beginning of the classical period onward Hindus seem to divide more and more into two large groups: those who follow Viṣṇu and those who follow Śiva. In the modern period there are among the Hindus numerous separate sects or churches dedicated to particular theologies of these great divinities. All adherents of Viṣṇu of whatever sect have the generic term Vaiṣṇava applied to them, while adherents of Śiva are called Śaiva. When we turn to the examples of Vaiṣṇava devotees, we discover that starting in the Buddhist period they begin to build a recognizable tradition of personal experience of God. Before examining this development in more detail, let us observe that a noticeable alteration in the form of Indian worship was a contributing factor to the changes which took place at the time devotional religion arises.

Vedic worship tended to have a somewhat mechanical character. At one level it was designed to produce consequences that would ultimately be of benefit to the worshipper's material well-being. It was also imbued with a sense of the complex design of the physical cosmos, whose personal aspect was set forth, but in a rather two-dimensional way.

We have already seen the situation in which the Upaniṣads witness the change from external to internal spiritual attention. At the same time the ordinary cult was changed rather differently. The Vedic sacrifices had been performed in the open air or in the *yāgaśālā* and had consisted largely in the ritual burning to the gods of food in various forms. From classical times onward, however, worshippers customarily offered their prayers either privately in their houses or in the precincts of temples, the architectural and sculptural embellishments of which grew increasingly elaborate in the later classical period.[16] The gods worshipped in these temples, especially Viṣṇu and Śiva, had become multidimensional. They revealed powerful personal characteristics but also had transcendental aspects, linked both with yogic ideas and the magical thought of the Tantric cult—probably the transformed and internalized Vedic cult with certain non-Vedic additions.[17] From the perspective of the growth of the cult of personal gods, one might consider the effect which the elaborate and courtly rituals, performed by staffs of priests, musicians, and dancers in the glamorous setting of ornate temples, must have had on the imaginations of the worshippers. It is not possible to trace these consequences in full. We do know, however, that for the devotees the gods had become real persons—grand, powerful, and, especially in the case of Viṣṇu, loving. The personal dimension of a god could thus be completely absorbing to a certain type of religious specialist.

Among such specialists were an obscure group of devotees who worshipped Bhagavān or Vasudeva, both epithets of Viṣṇu, and were called Bhāgavatas or Vasudevakas. They appeared about the third century B.C.E. and established what is called the Pañcarātra system, a method for worshipping Vasudeva. The technique they developed is presented in works bearing the name *Pañcarātra-Saṁhita* which we know partly through their limited publication and partly from references to their teachings in commentaries written by Rāmānuja and Śaṁkara on other works.[18] Śaṁkara records the fivefold method of worshipping Bhagavāt Vasudeva according to the teaching of the Bhāgavata school: *abhigamaṇa,* going to the temple of the deity with the body and the mind centered on him; *upādāna,* collecting the materials of worship; *ijyā,* worship; *svādhyāya,* the saying of mantras; *yoga,* meditation. "By worshipping him in these ways for a hundred years, all sin is destroyed and the devotee reaches Bhagavat."[19] Aside from such references as these, we have little information concerning the cult and history of the Bhāgavatas. It is about a thousand years after the Pañcarātra period before the Hindu *bhakti* specialization achieves a clearer historical form.

There is a saying in Sanskrit referring to the migration of *bhaktas,* followers of the *bhakti* tradition, or to the period of growth, development, and decline in the movement, as follows: "Utpannā Drāviḍe bhaktiḥ/ Vṛddhim Karṇāṭake gatā/ Kvacit kvacin Mahārāṣṭre/ Gurjare pralayaṁ gatā." It translates: "Bhakti began in the Dravida country, flourished in the Karnatak country, had so-so success in Maharashtra, and died out in Gujurat."[20] By the middle of the first Christian millennium, the main center of Vaiṣṇavism and of the resurgence of Hinduism (hand-in-hand with the decline of Buddhism) was in South India, where the Āḷvār saints flourished. The word *Āḷvār* refers to one who has a deep intuitive knowledge of God and one who is immersed in the contemplation of Him. The object of love of the Āḷvārs was Viṣṇu, upon whom they placed utter and complete *prapatti,* dependence.[21] The hymns they wrote in Tamil were love lyrics in which the devotee compared himself to a woman either immersed in or longing for union with the divine lover. In the outpouring of love for God there was little systematization. The Āḷvārs cannot be dated much before the seventh or eighth century C.E.[22] However, one must assume that sufficient time had passed for the establishment of the tradition, based on their experience, which was then carried north in the writings of the later Vedāntist philosophers and developed further by the writers of vernacular poetry.

The writings of the Āḷvārs are significant for their impassioned descriptions of ecstasy in the presence of and extreme sorrow in separation from Vasudeva, the ideal of their erotic mysticism. Their devotion did not emphasize the need for perfecting the soul of the devotee or of acquiring special merits through deeds of various sorts. Instead Vasudeva bestowed his love on those aspirants who surrendered to him completely, even though such an experience of divine communion was not always easy to achieve. In fact, as in Indian secular love poetry, the heart and soul of the Āḷvār were consumed with pangs of separation or *viraha.* One of the greatest among the Āḷvārs, called variously Nāmmāḷvār or Śaṭhakopa, is described by S. N. Dasgupta: "The feeling of devotion to God felt by Śaṭhakopa could not be contained within him, and, thus overflowing, was expressed in verses which soothed all sufferers. . . . Śaṭhakopa's main ideal was to subdue our so-called manhood by reference to God *(puruṣottama),* the greatest of all beings . . . as but [our being] women dependent on Him."[23] The Āḷvār "not realizing God in communion . . . feels a bond of sympathy with all humanity sharing the same grief."[24]

There arose a class of writers and orators, the Vaiṣṇava *ācāryas,* in descent from the Āḷvārs or under the influence of their ideas. Their first writer of historical renown was Nāthamuni. He was followed by Yāmunācārya, whose famous disciple was Rāmānuja (born around 1118), the great hero of the dualist faith.[25] Rāmānuja used the same general authorities as the monists, the Upaniṣads and the *Brahma Sūtra,* to establish his belief in the threefold nature of reality: "The individual or animal soul *(Cit),* the insensate world *(Acit),* and the Supreme Soul *(Īśvara).*[26] Also using terms and ideas from Sāṁkhya philosophy and certain Upaniṣadic texts, he devised the following five modes for Īśvara: (1) as *Parabrahman* or *Paravasudeva* he lives in Vaikuṇṭha, the heavenly abode where he is surrounded by the spirits of the delivered; (2) as *Vyūha* he has assumed the four principal forms of the godhead, Vasudeva, Saṁkarṣaṇa, Pradyumna, and Aniruddha; (3) *Vibhāva* refers to the state of the ten *avatāras;* (4) as *Antaryāmin* he dwells in the heart and "accompanies" the eternal souls; (5) he abides in images after a spiritual manner.[27]

For Rāmānuja the souls of men were eternal, self-illuminated, and unchangeable. They differed from God in their essential mode because they were subject to God's control and depended on God for their existence. Although some later writers comparing the texts of the Rāmānujists with those of the Āḷvārs have discovered variations in their fundamental notions, nevertheless they were agreed that *prapatti* or self-surrender to God was the essential attitude of the devotee. "Such a devotee feels that the Lord *(svāmī),* being the very nature of his own self, is to be depended on under all circumstances. This is called the state of supreme resignation *(nirbharatva)* in all one's affairs."[28]

The next important philosopher, Madhva (1197–1273 C.E.), espoused an explicitly dualistic philosophy. He wrote a commentary on the *Brahma Sūtra* and other works and was deeply influenced by the Purāṇas, particularly the *Bhāgavata Purāṇa.* In other ways his point of view was more strictly dependent upon faith in the scriptures, especially the Vedas. These he interpreted as revealing that Brahman is *saguṇa,* with qualities, as opposed to *nirguṇa,* without qualities, and that each one of his qualities is boundless. "He is the author of the eight acts of creation, preservation, destruction, governance, knowledge, ignorance, bondage and release."[29] Madhva taught that when the free soul achieves release, *jīvan-mukti,* it does not lose its self-identity. This contrasts strongly with the monist view that the salvation of the self consists in recognition of identity, hence loss of self-identity, in the Absolute. The followers of Madhva grouped themselves into a sect or *sampradāya* called the Brahmā, sometimes *Sad-Vaiṣṇava.* Other Vaiṣṇava *sampradāyas* include the Sanakādi, founded by Nimbāditya; the Śrī, founded by Rāmānuja; the Vallabha Sampradāya, founded by Vallabhācarya; and the Rādhāvallabha Sampradāya, founded by Śrī Hit Harivaṁś.

The philosophy of Vallabhācarya, together with the theology of the Caitanya sect and that of the Rādhāvallabha Sampradāy, evidences a final development in *bhakti* thought.[30] Vallabha's system is known as *viśuddhādvaita,* "pure Advaita." Although this teaching is, from the point of view of the human soul, distinctly dualist, the insistence upon maintaining a connection with Śaṁkara is evidence for the prestige in this link with the main exponent of Vedānta philosophy. For Vallabha, the Supreme is Kṛṣṇa, who is identified with the Brahman of the Vedas. Thus the *saguṇa* form of Brahman is superior to the *nirguṇa,* but Kṛṣṇa is both. He manifests himself as the *Antaryāmin,* the principle that dwells in individual souls, and as *Akṣarabrahman,* both cause and expression of the phenomenal world. For Vallabha the *advaita* aspect of Kṛṣṇa consists in his identification with the manifested world, in which he is as fully present as in the heart of the Godhead. However, the souls or *jīvas,* completely dependent upon God, remain distinct from him. In this framework *bhakti* reigns supreme.

> The state of *bhakti* when we enjoy God with all our senses and mind is even better than *mokśa. Bhakti* for Vallabha is *prema* and *sevā,* love and service. Through intense attachment to the Supreme one perceives him in all things, for they are all manifestations of God. In attaining the highest form of *bhakti, Śuddha-puṣṭi-bhakti* (pure-sustenance or enjoyment—*bhakti*), the soul is admitted to the eternal sports of Kṛṣṇa. The *bhakta* is transported to Vṛṇdāvan where he may become a tree or a bird, a cow or a beast, or he may become a cowherd or Gopī and enjoy Kṛṣṇa's dance. A corollary of this teaching was the life of the . . . Sampradāy, founded by Vallabha, whose chief deity was the Child Kṛṣṇa, represented by a beautifully clothed image and honored by daily ceremonies.[31]

Vallabha's teaching is also called *puṣṭimārga,* the path of enjoyment, indicating that the savoring of Kṛṣṇa's *rasa* is the chief consideration therein.

In the teaching of Caitanya, especially as interpreted through the six *gosvāmīs* of Vṛṇdāvan, the erotic mode, *śṛṇgāra* or *madhura,* is fully developed. The relationship between Rādhā and Kṛṣṇa is of paramount concern. Both the legitimacy of the relationship (if *svakīyā,* then Rādhā and Kṛṣṇa are legally married; if *parakīyā,* then they are not) and the question of whether the *rasa* is greater from the licit or illicit are examined, as well as the constancy of the relationship, with the emphasis falling on the side of *viraha,* or love in separation. According to Baladeva Vidyābhūṣaṇa, one of the *gosvāmīs,* there are five elements in the main teaching of the sect: *Īśvara, jīva, prakṛti, kāla,* and *karma.* Śrī Kṛṣṇa is infinite power, possessing the qualities of *saccidānanda.* To the extent that man is separated from Kṛṣṇa he is deprived of that transcendent state.

> Liberation is obtained through the grace of the Lord. In the state of liberation the being remains distinct from Brahma. Devotion constitutes the only

> means of reaching the highest *puruṣārtha*. There are three phases in the path of devotion: *sādhana, bhāva* and *prema*. *Sādhana bhakti* is that which is obtained thanks to the senses. This *bhatki* activates the love which exists in the heart of the [human] being and thus bears the name, *sādhana-bhakti*. *Bhāva* is the phase that precedes love. When *bhāva* is intensified, one calls it love *[prema]*. Love is the final result of effort. Love is the eternal dharma of the being and constitutes the ultimate *puruṣārtha*.[32]

Through the developments in theism—in this case the worship of Viṣṇu and his avatars—we can trace a movement from the efforts of the Upaniṣadic writers to understand the fundamental nature of the universe on through a theological evolution leading to the later devotion to Kṛṣṇa and Rādhā. Besides alluding to the poets, philosophers, and theologians who contributed to these changes, I shall briefly indicate the influence of certain writings that helped to create the climate in which the *bhakti* movement then developed its specific characteristics.

Primary Literature

Probably the most important work in the literature of *bhakti* is the *Bhagavad Gītā*. This exposition of various themes inherent to the Hindu religious outlook can be viewed from different perspectives, but surely Franklin Edgerton is correct in speaking of *bhakti* in the *Bhagavad Gītā* as "the most cardinal doctrine of the poem."[33] The central chapters of the work emphasize *bhakti* while the earlier and later sections treat other themes. Chapter IX clearly represents the worthiness of the ideal of *bhakti*. In describing the devotee it says, "Ever glorifying Me, And striving with firm resolve, And paying homage to Me with devotion, Constantly disciplined, they wait upon Me" (14).[34] And further, "A leaf, a flower, a fruit, or water, Who presents to Me with devotion, That offering of devotion I Accept from the devout-souled [giver]" (26). Although it would be difficult to say precisely to what extent the *Bhagavad Gītā* directly influenced the writing of *bhakti* poetry in North India in the Middle Ages, it was nevertheless a principal source for devotion to Viṣṇu from the pre-Christian era onward.

Another scripture of the devotional movement is the collection of the *Bhakti Sūtras* of Narada. These were composed by the twelfth century C.E., when the common imaginative themes of the Rāmite and Kṛṣṇite legends were well known. The *Bhakti Sūtras* constitute a technical work, a scientific treatise on the nature of *bhakti* and how to experience union with God through this spiritual discipline. In all, the eighty-four apothegms or *sūtras,* amplified by commentaries, formalize the devotional experience so that it can be considered in a conventional or philosophical way.[35] Its influence was widespread in the medieval period and contributed to aspects of the poetic statements of various medieval writers.[36] It also helped to clarify for the Indian mind the steps by which a spiritual aspirant, following the technique of *bhakti,* reached his goal.

An important form in the background of the devotional movement is a certain religious scenario—a mythological statement of the saving acts of the avatar of God. This is particularly true for the Rāmite and Kṛṣṇite *bhaktas*. (It would scarcely be true for the so-called *nirguṇa bhakti* wherein such writers as Kabīr eschewed anthropomorphization.) The suggestive power of the life story of the avatar of God is seen in the strong influence of the *Bhāgavata Purāṇa* throughout the late classical period and into the Middle Ages, providing inspiration for the various sects of Kṛṣṇa. Sections of the work relate to the charming play of the infant Kṛṣṇa,[37] however, the scripture also elaborates on the love between Kṛṣṇa and the *gopīs* or cowmaidens. In this setting the *śṛṇgāra* or erotic mood is very pronounced. A thirteenth-century poem, the *Gīta Govinda* of Jayadeva, develops the story of the love between Kṛṣṇa and the *gopīs* to its highest state in Sanskrit poetry. Here the *gopī* Rādhā is identified for the first time by name as the favorite of Kṛṣṇa. The alternating states of separation and union experienced by the lovers provide inspiration for various sectarian interpretations in the sixteenth century that attempt to understand and explain the relationship between the soul and God on the basis of the Rādhā-Kṛṣṇa relationship. Both in his literary style and through the religious scenario of his writing Jayadeva influences the work of Śrī Hit Harivaṁś.

Related to these major literary works are anecdotal writings from various sources which show the way in which Viṣṇu has saved one of his devotees who has fallen into desperate circumstances. Although less applicable to the *bhakti* of erotic love, they help to create and sustain the general atmosphere of faith, and should be noted in this regard. Recalling these stories in their allocutions to the Lord, the poets and saints of the Middle Ages thus remind him that on a previous occasion he has saved his supplicants in a particular way—in spite of their weakness, sinfulness, or despair. The poets suggest to the Lord that they are even more worthy of salvation than an extremely great sinner or outstandingly pathetic creature from the past because in every way their sins and wretchedness surpass all others.[38]

In the later Middle Ages a work entitled *Bhaktamālā, Garland of Devotees,* appeared in Hindi under the authorship of Nābhādāsa, with commentary by Priyādāsa. It is a primary source which contains theological and biographical information concerning the beliefs and practices of the *bhaktas,* poets, saints, and devotees of the time. It also gives us perspective on the structural characteristics that arose from the synthesis of ideas that turned *bhakti* into a complex system of relationships between the devotee and God, thus becoming one of the major expressions of Hinduism. Drawing on the *Bhaktamālā* and other sources, G. A. Grierson was one of the first westerners to describe the way in which the *bhakti* theorists related the different aspects of devotion to the traditional *rasas* of Indian poetics. *Bhakti* was usually described under five categories, depending upon the "flavor" that was sensed in the relationship between God and man. "(1) The Resigned Flavour, *śānta rasa*. (2) The Obedient Flavour, *dāsya rasa*. (3) The Friendly Flavour, *sakhya rasa*. (4) The Tenderly Fond Flavour, *vātsalya rasa*. (5) The Passionately Loving Flavour, *śṛṅgāra rasa* or *mādhurya (madhura)* rasa."[39] The exact translations of these *rasas,* or the conditions from which they arise, the *bhāvas,* vary slightly in actual contexts. What is important is that the *bhakti* schools of devotees and writers tended to conform to these categories. We are concerned in this study with *śṛṅgāra rasa,* but some of the others gained a prodigious following, led to the creation of sects, and inspired the writing of striking literary works.

Literary Conventions

A rather surprising aspect of the development of the devotional movement in Vaiṣṇavism is the extent to which it no doubt depended upon literary theory and, particularly, on the poetic dimension in literary expression.[40] This is further related to the stylized manner in which criticism attempted to determine the origin of human emotions and their appropriate expressions. This approach is most clearly illustrated in the technical writings of the classical Indian theater, particularly in such works as the *Nāṭyaśāstra,* ascribed to Bharata Muni. In the *Nāṭyaśāstra* the author describes the permanent and temporary aspects of the principal human emotions, the main characteristics of the hero and heroine, and the way in which the dramatic art gives birth to the special quality of emotional expression which underlies the interaction between the *dramatis personae* and the spectators at the presentation of a play. Because these theatrical conventions have an important part in the writing of poetry and other types of Indian literature and were adapted to the theological statement of such *bhakti* poets as Śrī Hit Harivaṁś, some specific references will be made here.

It would no doubt have been impossible for the major *rasas* of *bhakti,* enumerated in the previous section, to have been expressed without the elucidation of the *Nāṭyaśāstra* and related works. At the same time, the particular experience of the *rasas* depended upon further refinements in the theory that gives rise to them. Overall, this was a normative, psychological theory. According to it, men experience up to forty-one different emotional states, *bhāva*-feeling; eight are fundamental or "durable," *sthāyin*. These last are love, mirth, sorrow, anger, energy, terror, disgust, and astonishment (called *sthāyībhāva*). The remaining thirty-three, including envy, intoxication, weariness, indolence, depression, anxiety, etc., are complementary to the *sthāyībhāva* and are called *vyabhicārin,* causal. These "play across" the former (which, when purely experienced, obliterate all other factors in consciousness) but have a less permanent character. In the theater, the spectator who witnesses the emotion experienced by the actor or actress, through its appropriate expression, does so in a peculiar manner as ". . . the relevant representation of the Durable Psychological State *[sthāyībhāva],* which is then called a Sentiment *[rasa].* The Sentiment, being a vicarious experience, does not affect him in any other way; and bringing in its wake a spiritual freedom, it may be said to purify his soul."[41] What determines the particular *sthāyībhāva* is the *vibhāva,* or the complex circumstance that provokes the emotion: this includes the *ālaṁban,* the object that arouses the emotion, and the *uddīpan,* the quality of the *ālaṁban*. The *uddīpan* is enkindled by the *vyabhicārībhāva*[42] as its cause. It is the *uddīpan* that is directly capable of arousing the *sthāyībhāva* in a particular subject or *āśraya*. The reaction of the *āśraya,* detected in its manifestations, is called the *anubhāva*.

The duty of the playwright and the actor is therefore to conduct the business of the drama so that the particular *rasa* is produced to the enjoyment or satisfaction of the spectator. In order for this end to be achieved the principal actors (and in dramas of the *śṛṇgāra* type there would be both hero and heroine—*nāyaka* and *nāyikā*) must correctly unite the *vibhāva* and *anubhāva* so that the *sthāyībhava* or *vyabhicārībhāva* may affect the spectator with *rasa*.[43]

Speaking now of the *bhakti* setting, this system requires the appropriate "scenario" for the intended effect, so that the *bhakta* may taste the divine *rasa* in the suitable manner. Even in the case of *śṛṇgāra rasa,* therefore, inventions of the poetic imagination, such as those expressed by Śrī Hit Harivaṁś, must be seen in this light. Indeed, the divinities Rādhā and Kṛṣṇa operate according to the rules of *bhāva,* and in doing so they call to mind the *nāyaka* and *nāyikā*. A final point is the role of "spectacle" in the theater of India and the literatures affected by it. Makeup, costuming, songs, orchestral pieces, and dances made important contributions toward evoking the *rasa*. We find that where it is appropriate to *bhakti,* the poet enlivens his descriptions of the divine beings and their milieu with many images that contribute to the reader's sense of the spectacle, the emotionally overflowing pageant of salvation.

The Historical Question

How important were the historical circumstances of the Indian Middle Ages in shaping the devotional practices of the mass of Hindus? Although it is easy to say that *bhakti* became popular as the oppression of Islām forced an inward and, at the same time, more informal style upon religious life, we cannot with any assurance declare that the devotional mood of the era was strictly a product of hard times. Provisionally, we must say that the *bhakti* movement was the final development of a long historical process, but that it required the emergence of the vernacular literatures to truly take hold of the popular imagination, and the creation of particular religious forms to suit divergent human temperaments. In the discovery of the precise idiom of the medieval devotional movement, the impetus of contact with the Muslim culture, and particularly with Sūfī mysticism, was very important.[44] In times when it was not possible to gather in the mysterious and glorious precincts of the great temples to witness the rites of the Sanskrit cult, devotees met privately in homes, as they do in India even today, to sing the praises of Rādhā and Kṛṣṇa in the poetry of their everyday speech and to receive in turn a taste of that deep joy and a feeling of the divine protection.

NOTES

1. The term is first used in its later, typical meaning in the *Svetāśvatara Upaniṣad* VI.23: *yasya deve parā bhaktiryasthā deve tathā gurau / tasyaite kathitā hyarthāḥ prakāśante mahātmanaḥ/* "These truths that have now been related shine forth [if they have been related to] a high-souled man who is possessed of 'bhakti' for [literally, on] God and for his guru as for a god." From "Bhakti," *Journal of the Royal Asiatic Society, Bombay* 23 (1908–1913): 109 ff. Cf. R. E. Hume, *The Thirteen Principal Upanishads,* 2d ed. (Madras: Oxford University Press, 1962), p. 411.
2. This may call to the reader's mind T. S. Eliot's definition of poetry: "Excellent words in excellent arrangement."
3. Quoted in Bharatan Kumarappa, *The Hindu Conception of Deity* (London: Luzac and Co., 1934), p. 19. For Vedic antecedents of these ideas, see H. Jacobi, *Die Entwicklung der Gottesidee bei den Indern* (Leipzig: Kurt Schroeder-Verlag, 1923).
4. Kumarappa, *Hindu Conception of Deity,* p. 20.
5. *Ibid.,* pp. 47–48.
6. V. S. Ghate, *The Vedanta* (Poona: The Bhandarkar Oriental Research Institute, 1960); M. Hunter, *Hindu Monism and Pluralism* (Bombay: Oxford University Press, 1932), especially chapters 6 and 7, which give important summaries and interpretations of the two major contrasting aspects of Indian thought.
7. J. Gonda, *Aspects of Early Viṣṇuism* (Utrecht: N. V. A. Oosthoek's Vitgerers Mij., 1954), p. 5.

8. *Ibid.,* p. 15.
9. *Ibid.,* p. 20.
10. *Ibid.,* p. 21.
11. *Ibid.,* pp. 13–24.
12. For the interpretation of this motif and its further incorporation into Buddhist mythology, see Mircea Eliade, "Les Sept Pas du Bouddha," *Pro Regno Pro Sanctuario* (Nijkeck: G. F. Callenbach, 1950), pp. 169–175.
13. Gonda, *Early Viṣṇuism,* p. 77.
14. *Ibid.,* p. 125.
15. In this connection see B. B. Bidyavinod, "Varieties of the Vishnu Image," in *Memoirs of the Archaeological Survey of India,* no. 2 (Calcutta: Superintendent Government Printing, India, 1920), for an excellent analysis of the iconic varieties indicative of Viṣṇu's divine aspects. See also Gopinath Rau, *Elements of Hindu Iconography* (Madras, 1914), I and II. For information on a wide variety of myths, consult V. Thomas, *Epics, Myths and Legends of India* (Bombay: D. B. Taraporeval Sons and Co., 1961). In addition to these works, see H. H. Wilson, *The Vishnu Purana, A System of Hindu Mythology and Tradition* (London: John Murray, 1840) and the summary provided in J. M. Macfie, *The Vishnu Purāna* (Madras: Christian Literature Society for India, 1926). Evaluations of the development of Vaiṣṇavite myths are found in Maurice Phillips, *The Evolution of Hinduism* (Madras: M. E. Publishing House, 1903), pp. 58 ff., and W. J. Wilkins, *Modern Hinduism* (Calcutta and Simla: Thacker, Spink, and Co., 1900), pp. 58 ff. For pertinent facts on typical Vaiṣṇavite worship see "On Vishnu and Siva Festivals," in M. M. Underhill, *The Hindu Religious Year* (Calcutta: Oxford University Press, 1921), pp. 75 ff. Other works that contribute to an understanding of Vaiṣṇavite imagery are Heinrich Zimmer, *The Art of Indian Asia, Its Mythology and Transformations,* ed. Joseph Campbell (New York: Bollingen Foundation, 1960), I and II, and Zimmer, *Myths and Symbols in Indian Art and Civilization,* ed. Joseph Campbell (New York: The Bollingen Foundation, 1963). Also see Alain Daniélou, *Hindu Polytheism* (London: Routledge and Kegan Paul, 1964).
16. For work on the Hindu temple, see especially Stella Kramrisch, *The Hindu Temple* (Calcutta: University of Calcutta, 1946).
17. The literature of Tantra is considerable. One might begin with W. T. Elmore, *Dravidian Gods in Modern Hinduism* (Hamilton, New York: privately published, 1915), for transitional forms. Also see Mircea Eliade, *Yoga,* Bollingen Series LVI (New York: Pantheon Books, 1958), pp. 200 ff. Also, Sir John Woodroffe, *The World as Power* (Madras: Ganesh, 1966); *The Garland of Letters (Varnamālā)* (Madras: Ganesh, 1963); *Karpūrādistotra* (Madras: Ganesh, 1953); *Introduction to Tantra Shastra* (Madras: Ganesh, 1952). Cf. Agehananda Bharati, *The Tantric Tradition* (London: Rider, 1965).
18. Commentary on *Brahmasūtra* II. 2. 29–42. Cf. A. Govindacarya Swamin, "The Pāñcarātras or Bhāgavat-Śāstra," *Journal of the Royal Asiatic Society of Great Britain and Ireland* 1911: 935–961. Also E. W. Hopkins, "The Epic Use of Bhagavat and Bhakti," *Journal of the Royal Asiatic Society of Great Britain and Ireland* 1911: 727–738. See G. A. Grierson, "Bhagavatism or the Foundation of Brahmanism," in the *Indian Antiquary* 37: 253, for the founding of the Vasudeva religion, and Grierson, *The Monotheistic Religion of Ancient India* (1907) for a sometimes fanciful but always interesting "history" of the cult of Vasudeva and related matters. See also R. Garbe, *Die Bhagavadagītā* (1905), p. 23, for more of the same.

19. Commentary on *Brahmasūtra* II. 2. 42.
20. A. K. Majumdar, *Bhakti Renaissance* (Bombay:Bharatiya Vidya Bhavan, 1965), p. 32.
21. A technical discussion of this point and its relation to an early philosophical dispute as to the nature of grace is found in S. N. Das Gupta, *A History of Indian Philosophy,* 5 vols. (Cambridge: Cambridge University Press, 1961–1965), 3: 85 ff. Also see comments about *Markata-kiśōra-nyāya* in A. Govindacharya's article, *Journal of the Royal Asiatic Society of Great Britain and Ireland* 1910: 1103–1112.
22. See S. N. Das Gupta, *History of Indian Philosophy* 3: 64. A conservative estimate would place them sometime just prior to the eleventh century A.D. See R. G. Bhandarkar, *Vaiṣṇavism, Shaivism and Minor Religious Systems,* Collected Works of Sir R. G. Bhandarkar, vol. 4 (Poona: Bhandarkar Oriental Institute), p. 69. S. K. Aiyanagar, *Early History of Vaishnavism in South India* (London: Oxford University Press, 1920), gives a fairly detailed critique of Bhandarkar et al. on Āḷvārs.
23. S. N. Das Gupta, *History of Indian Philosophy* 3: 69–70. A. J. Appasamy, *Temple Bells* (London: Student Christian Movement Press, 1930) has examples of poetry expressing South Indian religious values. A thorough study of Śaiva *bhakti* theology and mysticism in South India is given in Mariasusai Dhavamony, *Love of God According to Śaiva Siddhānta* (Oxford: Clarendon Press, 1971).
24. S. N. Das Gupta, *History of Indian Philosophy* 3: 71.
25. For material about Rāmānuja and confrères see T. Rajagopala Chariar, *The Vaishnavite Reformers* (Madras: G. A. Gratesan & Co., 1909). Selections from Yāmuna are included in L. D. Barnett, *The Heart of India* (London: Murray, 1908). For the life of Rāmānuja, see S. K. Aiyanagar, trans., "Yatirājavaibhavam of Āndhrapūrana," *Indian Antiquary* 38 (1909), nos. 13–16: 129 ff.
26. Bhandarkar, *Minor Religious Systems,* p. 73.
27. *Ibid.,* pp. 76 ff.
28. S. N. Das Gupta, *History of Indian Philosophy* 3: 86.
29. S. Radhakrishnan, trans., *The Brahma Sutra* (New York: Harper and Brothers, 1960). Also see K. A. Narain, *A Critique of Madhva's Refutation of the Samkhya School of Vedanta* (Allahabad: Udayana Publications, 1964), and Narain, *An Outline of Madhva Philosophy* (Allahabad: Udayana Publications, 1962).
30. In Hindi the final "a" of *sampradāya* (Skt.) is dropped.
31. Charles S. J. White, "Kṛṣṇa as Divine Child," *History of Religions* 10, no. 2 (November 1970): 168.
32. N. Shukla, *Le Karṇānanda de Kṛṣṇadasa* (Pondichéry: Institut Français d'Indologie, 1971), p. 14.
33. Franklin Edgerton, trans., *Bhagavad Gītā,* 2 vols. (Cambridge: Harvard University Press, 1952), 2: 70.
34. Numbers in parentheses refer to numbered verses in Edgerton's translation.
35. A typical example of a modern translation of this work is the *Narada Bhakti Sūtras,* translation and commentary by Swāmī Tyāgīsananda (Madras: Śri Ramakrishna Math, 1955). Also cf. "Bhakti," *Encyclopedia of Religion and Ethics,* and the unsigned article on *bhakti* in *Journal of the Royal Asiatic Society, Bombay* 23 (1910): 115, attributed to Mr. Sedgwick. An early definition of *bhakti* is found in H. H. Wilson, *Asiatic Researches* 18: 132. An inspiring

analysis of the meaning of *bhakti* for modern man is found in Swami S. D. Ramayanda's *Bhakti Yoga* (London: L. N. Fowler & Co., 1935). He states that "While the study of Raja Yoga demands the absolute individualization of the student, the study of Bhakti Yoga necessitates the total suppression of all personality in the student, so that his soul, animated by the power of the Spirit of God, can reach to great heights of holiness" (p. 14). See Charles S. J. White, "Bhakti," *Encyclopaedia Britannica,* 1964.

36. The commentary on *sūtra* 82 in Narada, *Bhakti Sūtra,* gives this elaboration of the varieties of *bhakti:* "Bhakti, or Divine Love, though in itself one only manifests itself in the following eleven different forms: (a) Love of the glorification of the Lord's blessed qualities, (b) Love of his enchanting beauty, (c) Love of Worship, (d) Love of constant remembrance, (e) Love of service, (f) Love of Him as a friend, (g) Love of Him as a son, (h) Love of Him as that of a wife for her husband, (i) Love of self-surrender to Him, (j) Love of complete absorption in Him, (k) Love of the pain of separation from Him."

37. For a summary of the relevant material on Child Kṛṣṇa see White, "Kṛṣṇa as Divine Child," and David Kinsley, "Without Kṛṣṇa There Is No Song," *History of Religions* 12, no. 2 (November 1972): 149–180.

38. For examples of these anecdotes see Śrī Nandadulāre Vājapeyī, editor, *Sūrsāgar* (Nāgarīprācarini Sabha, Samvat 2015), I, especially the Vinaya section, pp. 1-72. In the same connection see G. A. Grierson's articles on the *Bhaktamālā* of Nābhā-dāsa, "Gleanings from the Bhakta-Māla," in the *Journal of the Royal Asiatic Society of Great Britain and Ireland* (1909: 607–644; 1910: 87–109; 1910: 269–306) and his discussion of the *Vinaya Pattrikā,* "The Book of Petitions," a series of forty-three hymns and prayers addressed to the lower gods of Rāma's court and to the deity, in the *Journal of the Royal Asiatic Society of Great Britain and Ireland* 1903: 454–455 and 457–458. Somewhat more technical theological points are discussed in G. A. Grierson's summary of *The Narayaniya and the Bhagavatas* (Bombay: at the British India Press, 1909), a reprint from *The Indian Antiquary.* Also see Sister Nivedita, *Cradle Tales of Hinduism* (Calcutta, 1922), and Nivedita and A. K. Coomaraswamy, *Myths of the Hindus and Buddhists* (New York: Henry Holt & Co., 1914). Various "lives of saints" continue to inspire the Hindu devotee. One might consult H. P. Shastri's *Saints of India* (London: Shanti Sadam Publishing Committee, 1944) for an example of a modern work in this guise. See also Charles S. J. White, "The Sāi Bābā Movement: Approaches to the Study of Indian Saints," *Journal of Asian Studies* 31, no. 4 (August 1972): 863–878, and "Swāmī Muktānanda and the Enlightenment through Śakti Pāt," *History of Religions (May 1974).*

39. G. A. Grierson, "Gleanings from the Bhakta-Mālā," p. 611.

40. It has been said that the Indian drama is a poem that is seen.

41. Manomohan Ghosh, trans. and ed., *The Nāṭyaśāstra,* 2d ed. (Calcutta: Manisha Granthalya Private Ltd., 1967), p. xxxvii.

42. For details see Ghosh, *Nāṭyaśāstra;* H. H. Wilson, V. Raghavan, K. R. Pisharoti, and A. C. Vidyabhushan, *The Theatre of the Hindus* (Calcutta: Susil Gupta, Ltd., 1955). For the elements of classical criticism applied to medieval Hindi literature see Rāmbahori Shukla, *Kāvya-Pradīp* (Allahabad: Hindi Bhavan, 1969).

43. Also called *saṁcārībhava.*

44. See also Charles S. J. White, "Sufism in Medieval Hindi Literature," *History of Religions* 5, no. 1 (Summer 1965).

Part II. Toward Interpretation of the *Caurāsī Pad* of Śri Hit Harivaṁś

How the female divinity Rādhā came to dominate a mythic scenario that was predominantly the realm of the benevolent male deity is a central and ultimately unresolvable issue. Its background can be traced without difficulty, for Indian religion from the beginning has been deeply commited to the deity in feminine form. From the pre-Aryan city of Mohenjodāro, the famous goddess motif of the seals is the prototype. Such a goddess of fertility continues her own history down into subsequent periods of Indian folk religion. We cannot be certain where the inspiration arises for the goddesses in the *Ṛg Veda:* Pṛthivī, Vāc, Śrī, Sarasvatī, and Indrānī, to name a few. And there is Uṣas, the popular goddess of the dawn, who rides in a chariot, drawn by red horses, and bestows bounty. "Oh, dawn, daughter of heaven, arise and bring us your riches and your opulent abundance. Shining and generous goddess, come with your treasures" (I. 58).[1]

The suggestive imagery of the bountiful nature of a beautiful goddess is complemented by the more dynamic view of the *śakti*—or feminine aspect—of a male god, which is functional in the universe while the male tends to be withdrawn. The variations on this motif assume radically different guises. The iconic form of Śiva *Ardhanārī* is explicit—the god's left half is shown as his feminine form, *Pārvatī.* The interaction of *puruṣa,* the hidden male spiritual entity, in the manifested feminine cosmos, *prakṛti,* of Sāṁkhya philosophy is a more subtle development.

In the goddess cults that arose in the later classical period and continue down to modern times, the consort of Śiva is popularly worshipped in her terrifying aspect as Durgā, Kālī, or Caṇḍī. In this guise she becomes either the warrior who defeats the demon who would destroy the cosmos, or she is time personified, the inexorable devourer of every material form, including man himself. There is no doubt truth in the symbolic grotesqueness of her attributes—a necklace of human heads, fangs, running blood—as an image of the objective cosmos. At the same time, it is through this goddess that man's ultimate good must be realized in the same way that to religious man there may seem to be a good that flows lovingly to him out of a sometimes terrifying cosmos.

When we go back in the history of the Indian goddess we find that the specific developments that produce the supreme deity, Rādhā, from Vaiṣṇava origins build on a type of eroticism which is sentimental and literary in its basis, and emotionally remote from the Tantric, Śaktic cult of terrible goddesses.

The literary history of Rādhā has been sketched in the work of modern

Indian scholars. Her origins do not appear to be as old as those of Kṛṣṇa, although there is the phrase *"stotram-rādhānām-pate"* in the *Ṛg Veda* in which the word *rādhānām* has been construed to refer to the goddess.[2] Rādhā is best known for her relationship with Kṛṣṇa but it is not certain when this is clearly established. Her birth or creation is variously explained: she is found by Vṛṣbhānu, her father, on sacrificial ground; she is born to the wife of Vṛṣbhānu; she emerges from the left side of Kṛṣṇa; she descends from heaven through the curse of Sudāma and incarnates as a *gopī.* Otherwise, she is the *Viśākhā* star, the *Mahākuṇḍalinī,* the *Prakṛti,* or *Hlādinī Śakti* of the Lord.[3]

Among the Purāṇas only the *Brahmavaivarta* and *Padma* specifically mention Rādhā.[4] The antiquity of both is subject to question. Rādhā seems to appear iconically at Pahārapur in the fifth century and in literature about the same time[5]—whereafter she is mentioned frequently as the favorite of Kṛṣṇa.[6] It is doubtful, though, that Rādhā is truly regarded as a religious personage at that early date. In both the *Viṣṇu Purāṇa* and the *Bhāgavata Purāṇa,* references are made to the favorite of Kṛṣṇa without specifying Rādhā as her name. On the contrary, the main initiators of the *bhakti* movement, the Āḷvārs, refer to Kṛṣṇa's sweetheart as Nappinnai.

In later times, when we begin to read the theological discussions concerning these divinities, we learn that Kṛṣṇa and Rādhā were thought to be *advaya,* not two but one.[7] Rādhā, the *hlādinī* power of Kṛṣṇa, is supreme, but she also represents the devotee with the deepest state of devotion.[8] However, in the Sakhī sect Śrī Kṛṣṇa is regarded as supreme, but like the followers of Śrī Caitanya they recognize that Kṛṣṇa's feminine aspect is of great importance.[9]

Kṛṣṇa himself is a blending of three principal characters or personalities—this is apart from his apotheosis in the *Bhagavad Gītā,* where he manifests directly both the immanental love and the transcendent grandeur of Viṣṇu. The *Bhagavad Gītā* character of Kṛṣṇa was present in the background of consciousness of contemporary sixteenth century devotees of Kṛṣṇa, but the *bhakta* actually turned to the more anthropomorphic divinity as an object of devotion in the Middle ages.

Kṛṣṇa appears first of all in the guise of the warrior, the folk hero of Dvāraka, whose life is one remarkable—though not always meritorious—adventure after another. It was in regard to his amorous exploits particularly that his second personality emerges. Kṛṣṇa is the insatiable lover, the most desirable male in India's epic and Purāṇic literature. In contrast with these two characterizations, the child Kṛṣṇa form unites the themes of hero and lover with the sentimental eroticism, disguised or overt, of the Indian male child who is the darling of all. Perhaps the child

Kṛṣṇa motif was the catalyst that combined the other two aspects and transformed them. Thus when Kṛṣṇa was manifested as divine lover to his devotees in the Middle Ages, he appeared as the brave, but supremely tender, adolescent paramour of the maidens of *Braj*.[10]

The Sakhī Sampradāy was founded by Haridās and has some connection with the sect founded by Nimbārk, which eventually accepted meditation upon the *rasa* of Rādhā as its main concern. Both these sects were contemporaneous with that of Śrī Hit Harivaṁś and similar to it in belief if not in all its practices. For the Sakhī Sampradāy the term *sakhī,* literally friend, refers to the female companions of Rādhā who assist her in preparing for the union with Kṛṣṇa and witness the love sport of the divine couple. Rādhā is *svakīyā,* the legitimate wife, and the supreme enjoyer of Kṛṣṇa to whom she is second. The *sakhīs* identify with Rādhā to share the *rasa* she experiences in her relationship with Kṛṣṇa. Compared with the Rādhāvallabha Sampradāy, the adherents of the Sakhī Sampradāy emphasize literal identification with the companions of Rādhā and have a different understanding of the role of Rādhā in the Rādhā-Kṛṣṇa relationship.[11]

Śrī Vallabhācārya, either because of his extremely fervent devotion to Kṛṣṇa or because of his positing of Kṛṣṇa's *hlādinī* power, does not refer directly to Rādhā. However, his son, Viṭṭhalnāth, the actual founder of the Vallabha Sampradāy, wrote poems in praise of Rādhā, and the poet Sūrdās, whose works are particulary revered in the Vallabha sect, wrote some of the most sensitive verses about Rādhā found in the Hindi language. For him Rādhā and Kṛṣṇa were of one mind and soul, but gave the appearance of being two for the benefit of their devotees. They were as much united as the tree and its shadow, eyes and tears, water and waves. Rādhā was the chief beloved and wife; Kṛṣṇa is under her power because of his love for her—though he remains the supreme and ultimate deity.[12]

Reviewing the origins of the Rādhā cult, we notice that some scholars are willing to find a relationship between the Vaiṣṇava deity and forms of Tantric and Śāktic practice. They argue that the love goddess of Vaiṣṇavism would, in some measure, be a sublimated form of the goddess who is central to the erotic cults of Śaivite origin.[13] In Buddhist Sahajayāna Tantrism, Rādhā and Kṛṣṇa are often treated as forms of Ratipati and Rati; Kāma, Madana, etc.[14] These influences may bear heavily upon the Rādhāvallabha Sampradāy:

> Such moreover are the Radhavallabhis who date from the end of the sixteenth century and worship Kṛṣṇa, so far as he is the lover of Radha and Sakhi bhavas those who identify themselves with the friend, that is to say,

> with Radha, who have adopted the costume, manners and occupations of women. These last two sects are in reality Vaishnavite Shakts among whom we must also rank a great many individuals and even entire communities of the Chaitanya, the Vallabhacharya and the Ramanandis.[15]

As we have noted earlier, the style of Vaiṣṇava eroticism is quite distinct and could not be derived entirely from Tantrism as such. The complex Vaiṣṇava ideology itself inevitably leads to the erotic ambiance of the later Rādhāvallabhite and other sectarian literatures. To establish fully a mode of analysis that takes into account both the religious history of the various sects of Vaiṣṇava *bhakti* and the history of Indian creative literature with its complex systems of figures-of-speech, such matters as emotions involving the love of *nāyaka* and *nāyikā,* the origin of the *Kāmaśāstra* literature, and the influence of that literature upon Vaiṣṇava faith are pertinent subjects for investigation. One can preliminarily catch a glimpse of the complexity of that matrix, for it yielded the *chef d'oeuvre* of late Sanskrit literature, the *Gīta Govinda* of Jayadeva, a primary source in Vaiṣṇava history. There the poet's intention seems to have been to create a perfect expression of the course and consummation of love for the most worthy human pair. In this work Rādhā appears distinctly from among the group of *gopīs* and displays those characteristics that will depict her in the Vaiṣṇava churches. Indeed, the poet says that his intention is to create, through his poem, a vehicle for inducing devotion to Hari.[16]

In summation, it seems that the erotic style of Sanskrit imaginative literature plus the numerous components that build up the Vaiṣṇava structure inspire the later generations of Vaiṣṇava poets. They incorporate this varied material uncertainly into the cult of Viṣṇu until the coming of the great devotional saints of the Middle Ages, who demonstrate that the imagery of erotic bliss can be faultlessly applied to the most sublime mystical apprehension of the divine nature—indeed, it is essential to its understanding.[17] Notwithstanding all this, to the extent that any system of *bhakti rasa* becomes a *yoga*—a discipline to achieve union with God—there may be a claim to a structural similarity between the *bhakti* of *śṛṇgāra rasa* and Tantric yoga. In both structures the given nature of sex is moved through religious means from one level of significance to another. In Tantric yoga sexual practice itself is changed; an effort is made to give the *yogi* the ability to control the sexual act in order to experience through it certain posited transcendental states. By means of disciplined meditation upon the sexual congress of divine beings, the *bhakti yogi* may also move beyond the literal image to a transcendent state. In both cases, it is the ability to control oneself in the framework of a proper motivation that is the key to success or failure. Both disciplines, to be effective, would have to be undertaken in the spirit of *vairāgya* or renunciation.

The Founder of the Rādhāvallabha Sampradāy

We have already discussed the gradual movement of the *bhakti* cult northward. Any interpreter of the *bhakti* cult in the Hindi-speaking area must examine the exact circumstances of the success of *bhakti* in the north and why such saints as Rāmānanda and Vallabha chose to settle there, virtually in the heart of the Muslim state, when they might have remained in the south relatively far from the Muslim center of power. Likewise, definitive data on Śrī Hit Harivaṁś must await further research. However, the general outlines of his life and work are available. The following is a summary of an oral report given to me by Hit Jīvan Gosvāmi in Vṛndāvan in February 1969. It contains minor additions, and comments on the teaching and religious practice of the sect.

> Śrī Hit Harivaṁś was born outside Vṛndāvan in a village on the Mathurā-Āgrā road. He was definitely a resident of the Mathurā district, which makes him unique among the *ācāryas,* or teachers of Vaiṣṇavism in Vṛndāvan. All the others had been born outside the district—including Śrī Vallabhācārya and the *gosvāmīs* of the Caitanya sect. He was born at the end of the fifteenth or the beginning of the sixteenth century, probably the *Ekādaśī* day of *Śukla* in the calendar month of *Vaiśākh, Samvat* 1559 (1503 C.E.). Harivaṁś was born in a village called "Bad" in the *Braj* area south of Mathurā, while his parents were traveling with the emperor from Delhi to Āgrā. His forefathers had lived in Deoband, Saharanpur district. His mother was Tārārāni, and his father, Vyās Miśra, was attached to the court of either Sikander or Bald Lodī as *Rājguru,* court astrologer. They were of the Gauḍ Brahmin caste. One of his uncles had been a *sannyāsī.*
>
> Because the family enjoyed the patronage of the royal court, Hit Harivaṁś was able to cultivate a mastery of *Braj Bhāṣā* and Sanskrit and could devote his whole time to religion. He grew up in Deoband. At five years of age he received a mantra directly from the goddess Rādhā, and some days afterwards at Rādhā's command he brought up from a well an image of the Lord with the name Raṁgīlāl and established it in Deoband where it is still worshipped. At eight years of age he had the Upanayana sacrament and in his eleventh year he was married to Rukmaṇī. While he lived the householder's life, he had three sons and one daughter. At thirty-two years of age Rādhā appeared to Harivaṁś in a dream; whereupon he left his home and travelled toward Vṛndāvan. Rādhā had told him that at a place called Carthāval there lived a brahmin named Aturdev. From him he would receive a *mūrti* of Rādhāvallabha [Kṛṣṇa] that should be the principal object of devotion in the sect. Harivaṁś met the brahmin, and when he had obtained the image he took it with him to Vṛndāvan.

In those days Vṛndāvan was a dangerous forest. There was a dacoit chief named Narvāhana living there. Harivaṁś first stayed at a place called Madhanter. When Narvāhana heard that a saint had come to the forest, he sent some of his men to tell Harivaṃś to go away; however, they were very impressed by the latter's shining appearance and returned to their leader without causing him any harm. Then Narvāhana himself came to see Harivaṁś. When he arrived, Harivaṁś was singing a verse from the *Caurāsī Pad*. When the dacoit heard the lines of sacred poetry, he broke into tears and asked Harivaṁś to become his guru and told the saint that he could live anywhere in the district without fear. The saint stayed on there for eighteen years; Narvāhana so changed his way of life that he, too, in time became a saint: Harivaṁś honored him particularly by granting him a vision of Rādhā.

There were four sampradāys in Harivaṁś' period: the Nimbārk, Rāmānuja, Madhva, and Vallabha. These all criticized Śaṁkara's *advaita* teaching. Harivaṁś, on the contrary, took no stand on the issue of *advaita*. His doctrine was very simple: that only through love can one achieve the ultimate spiritual bliss. Rādhā, Kṛṣṇa, the *sakhīs,* or female friends, and the forest of Vṛndāvan, these are the four aspects of love. All the other *ācāryas* said that the ultimate reality was Kṛṣṇa, but Harivaṁś said that although Kṛṣṇa is God, he, in turn, worships Rādhā, the supreme power of love; from Rādhā Kṛṣṇa begs for grace. The love of Rādhā and Kṛṣṇa does not partake of sexual desire. The verses of the *Caurāsī Pad* seem to be filled with eroticism *(śṛṇgār);* for Rādhā and Kṛṣṇa, sexual love in the literal sense is irrelevant. The point is that Rādhā and Kṛṣṇa are not different. They are two aspects of the same love, and hence they feel no personal desire in their love; rather, they wish only to fulfill the desires of others. Rādhā sacrifices herself for Kṛṣṇa; Kṛṣṇa sacrifices himself for Rādhā. The *sakhīs* witness this bliss and themselves are filled with bliss. The love of Rādhā and Kṛṣṇa is aimless and causeless for they themselves are the very essence of love.

One can make a distinction in the teaching of various works on the subject of love play and the bliss, *rasa,* of the union of Rādhā and Kṛṣṇa. In the *Bhāgavata Purāṇa* and in the writings that rely upon it, it appears that the love play of Kṛṣṇa with the *gopīs* and with his favorite mistress is only of short duration, and afterwards the participants experience separation from Kṛṣṇa. Such is not the case in respect to Harivaṁś' teaching. The love play and bliss of the divine couple is *nitya,* eternal. It is not limited by day or night, season, or place. Vṛndāvan, where Rādhā and Kṛṣṇa play and the *sakhīs* watch, is the very grounds of *rasa*. Even though it is in the world, it transcends the world. When Rādhā and Kṛṣṇa are pleased with their devotees, the world is converted into the divine Vṛndāvan. There Rādhā and Kṛṣṇa live forever. They are not in heaven; they are here on earth, present in the actual place Vṛndāvan as well as present to their devotees wherever they worship with faith—it is as though the whole earth becomes paradise when they are present.

In *śloka* 260 of the *Rādhāsudhānidhi,* Hit Harivaṁś writes that the Vedas and Purāṇas do not disclose Rādhā. No doubt Rādhā and Kṛṣṇa are not in the Vedas, but the grace of Vṛndāvan is such that Rādhā and Kṛṣṇa are shown to him who lives there. The *sakhīs* are witnesses of their love. If you want to worship Rādhā and Kṛṣṇa, you should seek Vṛndāvan for shelter. Hit Harivaṁś said, "I have no objection to other worshippers of God. Everyone can choose his own form of God; but as for me Rādhārānī is the ultimate God."

Hit Harivaṁś established four shrines, Sevakuṁj, Rasmandal, Vaṁśivat, and Mansarubar, which are the oldest shrines in Vṛndāvan. It was in his time that the statue of Rādhāvallabha was set up as we have it today. Harivaṁś went to Rasmandal in the evening and addressed his disciples. Vaṁśivat was the place where he took the image of Rādhāvallabha. Mansarubar was where he spent the nights in religious singing, *bhajan*. Dāmodardās, his principle disciple, believed that Hit Harivaṃś was God Himself—the *Guru.* Dāmodardās taught that Hit Harivaṁś contains Rādhā, Kṛṣṇa, the *sakhīs,* and Vṛndāvan. If we have seen Harivaṁś, we have seen all four aspects.

Today the disciples are initiated by being brought by the guru into the sanctuary of the main temple in Vṛndāvan where they are allowed to touch the image of Śrī Rādhāvallabha and are told the mantra. The mantra cannot be repeated to one who is not initiated. It consists of twelve words. Anyone who believes in the doctrines and is independently minded can be a member of the Sampradāy. The elder men of the families of *gosvāmīs* give *gurudīkśa* and teach the aspirants. They are direct descendants of Harivaṁś. Only *gosvāmīs* can worship the image, and they are the hereditary owners of the temples. Anyone can go and see the image from a distance. There are about eighty families of *gosvāmīs* and about five *lakhs* of followers found in all parts of India. The majority of the members live in Gujarat, Maharashtra, and Madhyapradesh, but they can be found in Rajasthan, Bihar, Bengal, Kashmir, Panjab, and other areas, also. The *gosvāmīs* marry only in the Gauḍ Brahmin caste, but their followers may marry in any caste which is appropriate to them. All receive *gurudīkśa,* irrespective of caste. The Rādhāvallabha *gosvāmīs* and the Caitānya *gosvāmīs* both belong to the Gauḍ Brahmin caste.[18]

Teachings of the Rādhāvallabha Sampradāy

The following are the main elements in the teaching and poetry of the sect:

a. Rādhā is the very ground of being. She is eternal power and the giver of bliss in the universe. Being absolute she is without form and qualities, and yet her devotees are her companions *(sakhī* or *sahacārī)* who adore her while she is amorously sporting with Kṛṣṇa. It is through

Rādhā's physical manifestation and the grasp of her psychological character that a devotee at length finds the route to her eternal aspect. The love play and the granting of all wishes and desires for the devotees are merely aids to that discovery. Rādhā is without equal in the universe for beauty, and her power constantly defeats the god of love, Kāmadeva. There are no negative emotions appropriate to her; hence she is without the characteristics of Devī or Śakti. Simply put, she is the goddess of love to Kṛṣṇa.[19]

b. Kṛṣṇa, the eternal young, lover deity enjoys *rasa*—the ecstasy of love—forever and is the only male participating in the love sport of Vṛndāvan. He, too, is the supreme Lord but functions as the sexual companion of Rādhā. In these amorous actions he arouses Rādhā who then releases the *sṛṅgāra rasa* to the devotees and to the world through the *rāsa līlā* and the bower sport. Kṛṣṇa has become incarnate in order to love Rādhā: one might almost say that by an inversion of the usual symbolism Kṛṣṇa becomes Rādhā in her male aspect; the two divinities are often described in very similar terms.[20]

c. The *sakhīs* or *sahacārīs,* companions, represent the world of human incarnation, the *jīvas.* In the state of being *sahacārī,* sex and caste differences are obliterated and all are the eternal spectators and enjoyers of *sṛṅgāra rasa.* Therefore, the *sakhīs* are superior to the *gopīs* who knew the prolonged pangs of separation from Kṛṣṇa. To a certain extent they share the wifely status of Rādhā and can enjoy the sport with Kṛṣṇa; but their main function seems to be to assist in the meeting and union of Rādhā and Kṛṣṇa. From that union they receive bliss. Because they are important to Kṛṣṇa as go-betweens in arranging his meeting with Rādhā, Kṛṣṇa tries to please them, for without them the sport cannot take place. Like Rādhā and Kṛṣṇa they experience *sṛṅgāra rasa* with chaste minds and are completely pure and without any moral fault. All the companions are equal, although certain ones such as Lalitā are mentioned as being close to Rādhā.

d. Vṛndāvan is considered superior to Viṣṇu's heaven, Vaikuṇṭha. It is a place of great beauty and more desirable than Vaikuṇṭha, for Rādhā is present in the one and absent from the other. The setting of the love sport is described in profuse and ornate images in the *Bhāgavata Purāṇa* and *Padma Purāṇa,* but it is shown more naturalistically in the writings of Harivaṁś. To be in Vṛndāvan eternally is the chief wish of the devotee: to live and die, so to speak, in the unending bliss of the *rasa* sport.[22]

The *rasa* of *bhakti* can be savored in five different ways: devotion through resignation; devotion through service; devotion through friendship; devotion through parenthood; and devotion through passionate love.[23] Although each of these forms of *bhakti* is represented in the medieval literature, devotion through passionate love was considered the most perfect form. The Rādhāvallabha experience of *śṛṇgāra rasa* in the guise of *nityavihāra* takes one beyond all other possible experiences of *mādhurya bhakti*.[24] In its lower forms, as described in the *Bhāgavata Purāṇa* and *Viṣṇu Purāṇa,* and emphasized in the teaching of Caitanya and other devotees of Kṛṣṇa, it is held that Rādhā and Kṛṣṇa experience the polarities of separation, *viraha,* and union, *milana;* they are tormented by the experience of love under the guise of *parakīyā* (illicit heterosexual love) and its alternative *svakīyā* (legal heterosexual love) in which it is difficult to savor *śṛṇgāra rasa*.

The Rādhāvallabhīs claim that all these possibilities, with their good and bad points, are reconciled in the eternal sport of Rādhā and Kṛṣṇa. On the question of *viraha* versus *milana* the experience of the union of Rādhā and Kṛṣṇa is a very rapid and completely fulfilling alternation of these states.[25] Hence Kṛṣṇa experiences *viraha* in the most minute instances of separation—when he closes his eyes for a brief second and loses sight of Rādhā; whereas, the experience of *milana* is almost constant, and, moreover, it is without beginning and will be without end. The bliss of love-in-separation and love-in-union is transcended in their *nityavihāra*. The attention of the *sakhīs* is fixed upon the sexual congress of the divine lovers. For the female companions it is the source of sublime religious delight. In a sense there is nothing else of value in their world—Vṛndāvan, where the cool, gentle, sweet-smelling wind ever blows, has none of the distraction of what could be called historical change. The *sakhīs* live in the eternal present, the now of the consummate erotic experience wherein what they experience approaches the level of the bliss of Rādhā and Kṛṣṇa.

Although the details of the divine lovers' behavior are prefigured in the dramas and poetry of an earlier period and in the *Kāmasūtra,* the erotic description leads beyond such accidental characteristics to cause reflection upon the nature of the cosmos and the meaning of man's life.[26] Even if such reflections are not presented in philosophical discourses, the *nityavihāra* provides, through poetic statement, material for the meditations of such ascetic saints as Harivaṁś.

Though the terms and emotions are very different, it is not too far afield to surmise that the union of Rādhā and Kṛṣṇa takes place not only in terrestrial Vṛndāvan, a place the human devotee can aspire to visit, but also at the level of the cosmos. There Rādhā's function transverses and transcends all known and unknown dimensions of reality. It is no more impossible for Rādhā to assume the functions of such a universal deity and yet remain in her basic ideological expression within the Vaiṣṇava mode than it is for Viṣṇu himself to function as a universal deity without losing his distinctiveness, vis-à-vis Śiva, or as an *avatāra*.

The Cult of Rādhāvallabha

As we have already noted, the *bhakti* cults claim much greater freedom and informality for the devotee than the older strata of Hinduism from which they arose. Particularly in those periods of renewal under the inspiration and new teaching of a saintly *ācarya* or a poet—and such renewal continues to the present—there is the discovery of the freedom that comes in loving the chosen deity, or a human "god." In many of the sects that arose in the Middle Ages the tradition of freedom and informality is still asserted—especially when seen against the bondage of the "Vedic" expressions of ritual and, occasionally, social custom. At the same time, it appears that a standardized sectarianism exists in the major denominations of the *bhakti* cult; thus a priesthood, temples, image worship, elaborate *pūjā,* and the like occupy the day-to-day life of the devotees. Above all else, where the tradition of the sect provides for the composition of hymns or *bhajans* for group singing, such music becomes, through participation and/or understanding, a vehicle for the devotee to move beyond the external forms of the cult to an inner experience of ecstasy based on the intensity of his faith. Other elements in cultic life contribute to this kind of "reality" in the experience of the devotee. In the case of the Rādhāvallabha Sampradāy the imaginative reliving, on the very ground of Rādhā's love sport with Kṛṣṇa in Vṛndāvan, of the moment-to-moment bliss of the *nityavihāra* motivates the devotee more than the mere details of the temple, ritual, and seasonal festival. The external forms of worship must contribute to the constant recreation of that external experience.

In the main temple of the sect in Vṛndāvan the image of Śrī Kṛṣṇa, as Rādhāvallabha, was installed but with no corresponding image of Śrī Rādhā. Instead, the goddess is represented by the throne cushion or *gaddī,* an object regarded throughout Hinduism as a surrogate, nonliteral, image of a revered person or deity. According to Snātak, the *gaddī,* placed alongside the *mūrti* of Rādhāvallabha, has a golden leaf suspended over it upon which is written the name of Śrī Rādhā. Several reasons are given for service to Rādhā as the throne *(gaddīseva):*

First, Rādhā's beauty is indescribable (she is the Absolute and beyond all forms). Thus no icon would be suitable to represent her.

Second, Rādhā is a teacher; because the symbol of the teacher is the *gaddī,* the mind of the devotee should be fixed upon it.

Third, because Rādhā and Kṛṣṇa are engaged in eternal bower sport, if they were depicted together, this would have to be the main subject of the icon. It would be improper to depict them so, and it has been avoided; the devotee is enjoined to fix his attention mentally upon Rādhā through contemplating the *gaddī*. Devotion to Rādhā is further shown through writing her name on creepers, stones, and pieces of wood which are set up in various sacred places. (The name of Harivaṁś is similarly honored.)[27]

Public worship services are primarily the work of the *samāj,* who sing the songs of the *Caurāsī Pad* and other works by later poets of the sect appropriate to the season of the year and the time of day. The *Varṣotsava,* the yearly festival collection of such lyrics, is divided into six sections to correspond with the seasons.[28] To further honor Rādhā and Kṛṣṇa, daily courtly rituals and seasonal celebrations are held in temples in Vṛndāvan. There are seven daily services before the images:

Maṅgalā—6:00 A.M. The awakening of the deity and the offering of sweets, including butter and sugar lump. Stanzas three and thirteen of the *Caurāsī Pad* are sung. The *āratī,* or waving of lights in front of an image, is a feature of all hours of worship.

Śṛṇgar—10:00 A.M. The icon is bathed and adorned; various costumes are prescribed according to the day and season. Incense, curds, and sweets are offered. Stanzas nine and twenty-five of the *Caurāsī Pad* are sung.

Rājbhog—12:00 noon. The time of the main meal. Food offered to the deities consists of rice, curry, pulses, vegetables, curd, and sweets. Games such as *caupada* are played. From this time onward the songs sung at the hourly services are from works other than the *Caurāsī Pad.*

Utthāpan—4:00 P.M. The deities arise from the afternoon siesta. They are awakened with lute playing and bathing. Then dry and fresh fruits are offered together with incense. The deities go for their evening stroll.

Sandhyā—6:00 P.M. Various sweets are offered and there is singing, together with the *āratī.* The *rāsa* sport begins at this time.

Śayan—8:00 P.M. The evening meal of fried foods, *purī, halvā, rahanī,* and other dishes is taken. The *rāsa* sport continues.

Śaiyā—10:00 P.M. The time of retiring for the evening.[29]

In addition to the daily schedule there is a calendar of annual feast days. At first there were ten of these festivals, but as time passed more have been added, especially the birthdays of the famous *gosvāmīs.* The original ten festivals are as follows:

Phāgu—Holī	Pāṭ Utsav—Throne
Ḍol—Drum	Dīpamālikā—Lamp
Candan Vasan—Sandal Garment	Vanvihār—Forest Sport
Tīj Hiṁdol Jhul—Swing	Khicarī—Rice
Śarad—Autumn	Vasant—Spring[30]

Signs of the cult include the use of a *tilak,* or forehead mark, consisting of a curved loop with a dot in the center. The loop comes down close to the bridge of the nose and is said to symbolize Kṛṣṇa, the loop, and Rādhā, the dot. Preferably it is made of sand from Rādhākuṇda, a place in the Braj area. A rosary with an unfixed number of *tulsi* beads is made of two threads, Rādhā and Kṛṣṇa, wound together.[31]

There is another aspect of worship to discuss if we take the word worship in a very broad sense. We know of the love relationship between Rādhā and Kṛṣṇa from the *Bhāgavata Purāṇa, Viṣṇu Purāṇa,* and other sources. Moreover, we can see clearly in the *Gīta Govinda* and the *Caurāsī Pad* the way this material was transformed into a literary meditation. Because their code of morals usually was family-oriented, the Vaiṣṇavas would have to find ways and means to avoid being drawn into the erotic attitudes and behavior of the Tantrics and others whom they did not wish to emulate. We find in the history of *Kṛṣṇabhakti* that a considerable theological effort has been made to determine whether Rādhā was Kṛṣṇa's wife or his mistress. For a large number of Vaiṣṇavas, including the followers of Harivaṁś, the erotic descriptions were no doubt acceptable only if they were thought to derive from the married state.

However, in spite of the various refinements which the philosophers and the poets themselves brought to the understanding of their love poems, there were trends in the Vaiṣṇava sects which literalized some of the imagery. In certain sects there may have been actual sexual intercourse performed to stimulate the same act of the divinities. In the sect of the Sakhībhāva the male members began to wear female attire as a regular practice and tried to achieve total identification with Rādhā or the companions. For the most part, though, such extremes were avoided.

It seems evident that it was Śrī Hit Harivaṁś who transmuted the natural tendency toward literalism, what Eliade would call the infantilization of the myth, into artistic expression. We owe to him the creation of the first company of *rāsa līlā* performers, who through depicting the stories of the *Bhāgavata Purāṇa* in a kind of folk drama found a socially and artistically useful way of expressing the religious impulse to recreate the events narrated about the lives of the divinities.

According to the most reliable evidence, Hit Harivaṁś probably arranged the first of these performances. Other saints and poets thereafter contributed to the development of the genre, but it is worth noting that even today the Rādhāvallabha Sampradāy maintains what is considered to be the oldest *rāsa* troupe. It gives its plays in *Braj Bhāṣā* and incorporates material from the *Caurāsī Pad* and the writings of other poets as well.[32]

Hindi Literature

Before turning to the writings of Śrī Hit Harivaṁś, let us glance for perspective at some of the leading characteristics of the history of Hindi literature. It can be divided into four periods.

The first, or Vīrgatha Kāl, period begins around 1000 C.E. and lasts until 1400 C.E. During that time, the values of the warrior class were expressed in the two guises of *śṛṇgāra rasa* and the martial or *vīra rasa*. In the dialect of the writing, Diṁgal, an old form of Rajasthāni, *vīra rasa* predominated over *śṛṇgāra rasa* and reflected the mood created by the division of western India at the time into numerous small warring kingdoms. Hindus hold that it was this divisiveness which led them more and more to give way before the onslaught of the Muslims, who had established nearly complete hegemony in the region by 1400. This was the age of bardic or *caraṇ* literature, which is also called *Rāsa Sāhitya,* of which the most famous examples include the *Prithvirāj Rāso* and the *Ālhā Khand.* Writing at that time, the great Amīr Khusro helped develop the foundations of modern Hindi. From the same period, Vidyāpati's love lyrics on the Rādhā-Kṛṣṇa theme, collected in his *Padāvalī,* are formative for the centuries-long development of that genre in Hindi.

The second, Bhakti Kāl, the period of devotional literature (1400 C.E.–1700 C.E.), is generally regarded as a golden age during which some of the most famous and most beautiful works in Hindi literature were written. Two broad philosophical currents run through the writings of the time. The one stems from monistic antecedents and emphasized the *nirguṇa* or nonrelative nature of the Godhead as that most suitable for devotion. Poets like Kabīr emphasize the need to follow the *jñāna mārga,* the path of knowledge, and oppose sects, rituals, and anthropomorphic trends of all kinds in leading man to God. Similarly, the Sūfīs—of whom the greatest writer in Hindi may have been Mālik Muhammad Jaisi, famous for his *Padmāvatī*—used rich allegory and symbol to guide the spiritual aspirant through the phenomenal world to the Absolute. Sūfī literary works often made little distinction between what was Hindu and what was Muslim.

The dualist tendency, on the other hand, found its theological underpinnings in emphasis upon the *saguṇa* form of God, the God with qualities. Here the poets wrote on the theme of Kṛṣṇa or Rāma, with specialized theological developments, as in the case of Harivaṁś, dependent upon individual genius or interpretation. Of the works devoted to Kṛṣṇa, Sūrdās's *Sūrsāgar* is perhaps the most fully realized. Sūrdās is one of a group of poets called the Aṣṭacāp, followers of Vallabhācarya and his son Viṭṭalnāth. (The complete list includes Sūrdās, Kumbhadās, Paramānandadās, Nandadās, Kṛṣṇadās, Caturbhujadās, Citaswāmī, and Govindaswāmī.) As I have pointed out, Harivaṁś is closely allied to the Vaiṣṇava schools that have Kṛṣṇa as the chief deity—the difference being that Harivaṁś extols Rādhā above Kṛṣṇa. Numerous poets wrote on the theme of Kṛṣṇa and/or Rādhā, but only a few, like Sūrdās and Harivaṁś, expressed their devotion in the most masterful poetic form.

The poetic devotees of Rāma were also prolific. Great numbers wrote on the various themes that came originally from the *Rāmayāna* of Valmikī, but, at least in the Hindi area, few could compare with Tulsīdās, whose *Rāmcaritmanas* is sometimes hailed as the supreme masterpiece of the Bhakti period.

The third, or Rītī Kāl, period predominates from 1700 C.E. into the middle of the nineteenth century. The Bhakti spirit seems to give way more and more to an emphasis upon the technique of poetic expression. As we are indicating here, the interplay between the technique of poetic expression and its content—in the Middle Ages an often deeply felt devotion to God—must be grasped to appreciate fully the genius of a writer such as Tulsīdās or Harivaṁś. In the Rītī Kāl period the subject matter of poetry became considerably devoid of devotional emotion. The *śṛṅgāra rasa* for its own sake—the erotic for the erotic—largely prevailed as the search for even greater refinement in expression became a chief concern. In this somewhat limiting framework there were, nevertheless, great poets such as Bihārīlāl, whose *Satsaī,* "seven hundred verses," exhaustively and exquisitely demonstrated the technique of poetic expression on the subject matter of Rādhā and the *nāyaka* and *nāyikā*.

During the fourth period, from the nineteenth century onward under foreign rule, Hindi develops away from the medieval speech of Braj and Avadhī, and in the literary dialect of Khaḍi Bolī takes on the character of a modern language, the bulk of whose written expression is in prose. Yet distinguished poets as well as novelists and essayists have expressed themselves in this newer form of language.

The Literary Works of Śrī Hit Harivaṁś[33]

The works of the North Indian literary figures of the Middle Ages did not come under critical analysis until recent times. Unfortunately, the authorship even of some very important writings is now quite uncertain. The situation of Śrī Hit Harivaṁś, although somewhat better than those of others—his literary production was not so large and his main texts have undergone little apparent change since they left their author's pen—is a case in point. His six known works are *Śrī Hit Caurāsī Pad* and *Sphuṭvāṇī* (both in Hindi); *Rādhāsudhānidhi* and *Yamunāṣṭaka* (both in Sanskrit); and two letters in Hindi written to his disciple, Viṭṭhaldās. For some time there has been debate as to the proper title of the *Caurāsī Pad*. F. E. Keay and others identified it with a work called *Premlatā,* but it seems likely that a composition of that name is the product of Dhruvdās, a later member of the sect. Further doubts have been raised by those who note that some verses of *Caurāsī Pad* appear in the *Sūrsāgar Sār;* hence, the claim has been made that the former might be the work of Sūrdās. Such incorporations into Sūrdās are probably not rare and, until a definitive edition of *Sūr* appears, they afford no basis for the assumption that the verses in question are not the work of Harivaṁś. There are a few anonymous verses written in Harivaṁś' style with the signature line, "Jai Śrī Hit Harivaṁś," but these are probably the creations of enthusiastic devotees. In the case of the *Rādhāsudhānidhi,* the Caitanya sect tried to appropriate the work by adding a beginning and an ending verse in praise of Caitanya, and proposing that it had been authored by Śrī Prabodhānanda Sarasvatī.

The letters. These are brief spiritual instructions that emphasize the role of Rādhā as teacher and establish the personal affection of Harivaṁś for his disciple, Viṭṭhaldās, the Dīvān of Junāgadh.

Sanskrit works. The *Rādhāsudhānidhi* eulogizes Rādhā in the sect's typical manner. It resembles the *Caurāsī Pad* in its style and content, reiterates the fact that it is to Rādhā that devotion must ultimately go, and teaches that one cannot find Kṛṣṇa apart from Rādhā—if Kṛṣṇa is the moon, then Rādhā is the moon's light. Many of the same effects are sought in the two works; thus the bower sport is described as well as certain details such as Rādhā seeing her own reflection in the *kaustubhmaṇi* on Kṛṣṇa's chest. Moreover, emphasis is placed upon the power of Rādhā's name; the *sakhīs* are advised to invoke the name of Rādhā, as are *yogīs* and the gods themselves, to obtain some part of her bliss. She is the giver of joy, the preserver of the world. She is flawless in beauty and the very image of love, affection, and fondness. Kṛṣṇa is never put above Rādhā. The sight of the divine couple engaged in love sport is the most desirable experience in life. The *sakhīs* wish to press the feet of Rādhā and bathe and feed her in the morning when she has retired from the bower. Vṛndāvan, too, is described as the most beautiful possible paradise and the most desirable place to be born.

These examples from Growse's partial translation will give one a taste of the style and content of this work:

> 2. Hail to the majesty of Vrisha-bhānu's daughter, the holy dust of whose lotus feet, beyond the conception of Brahma, Siva and the other gods, is altogether supernaturally glorious, and whose glance moistened with compassion is like a shower of the refined essence of all good things.
>
> 4. I call to mind the dust of the feet of Rādhikā, which the noble milkmaids placed upon their head and so attained an honour much desired by the votaries of the god with the peacock crest, dust that like the cow of heaven yields the fullness of enjoyment to all who worship with rapturous emotion.
>
> 5. Glory to the goddess of the bower, who with an embrace the quintessence of heavenly bliss, like a bountiful wave of ambrosia, sprinkled and restored to life the son of Nanda, swooning under the stroke of love's thousand arrows.
>
> 7. When shall I become the handmaid to sweep the courtyard of the bower of love for the all-blissful daughter of Vrisha-bhānu, among whose servants oft and again every day are heard the soft tones of the peacock-crested god?
>
> 16. When, O Rādhā, will you fall asleep, while my hands caress your feet, after I have tenderly bathed you and fed you with sweet things, wearied with your vigil through a night of dalliance in the inmost bower, in the delicious embrace of your paragon of lovers?
>
> 19. Blessed Rādhika, cool me with the multiplicity of love that breathes in the swan-like melody of the girdle that binds your loins reddened with dalliance, and in the tinkling of the bangles, like the buzzing of bees, clustered round your sweet lotus feet.[34]

The *Yamunāṣṭaka* consists of eight *ślokas* and is written on the theme of the excellence of the river Jamunā (Yamunā), which has been compared to a beautiful woman. Commentaries have been written on both of these Sanskrit compositions.

Hindi works. Śrī Hit Caurāsī Pad,[35] the major writing of the poet and the leading text of the Sampradāy, is considered the best poetic composition. The stanzas together do not tell a story; instead each is an independent unit, although there is a unity between stanzas on the basis of their common themes. Among these themes we may speak of the *tat-sukhībhāva* character of the Rādhā-Kṛṣṇa relationship: it was essentially of the character to find its happiness in the happiness of others. The first line of the *Caurāsī Pad* illustrates this theme:

Whatever the Beloved does seems
Pleasant to me. Whatever seems pleasant
To me the Beloved does.[36]

Not only do they find happiness in giving love and bliss to each other but the very thoughtlessness of their mutual love illustrates its *advaya* character. So the poet asks in the final line, "Who pray tell can separate waves from water?" The mutuality and selflessness of the love is a benefit reaped by the devotees; in stanza thirty-two the poet says, after observing the lovemaking of the divine pair, "Today all limits are breached/ I offer myself as sacrifice in their immaculate retreat." This line reminds us of *pad* fifty-seven, where the *sakhīs* have been watching the lovemaking in a swing. Harivaṁś says here:

The hearts of her own
Well-wishing maids
Cannot contain their bliss:

Having gazed excessively with their eyes
(Their happiness having burst all bounds),
They threw themselves away![37]

The *tatsukhībhāva* love enables the devotee to abandon himself, lose himself in a marvelous rapture that intends to approximate the rapture and self-loss of the divine couple. We have already touched on the *nityavihāra* character of this work; the eternal sport makes it possible for the *tatsukhībhāva* to be continuously realized.

Before further discussion of the poetry's technical character, it is important to note the following points: Rādhā's beauty is the subject of several stanzas, including numbers twenty-nine and forty-five. One of the poetic devices throughout the poem is the contrast of the colors and attributes of the lovers. Kṛṣṇa is always dark, compared sometimes to a cloud, sometimes to a sapphire (or emerald), while Rādhā is fair, a flash of lightning, a golden lotus, a white swan. When the two make love, it is like a band of gold stretched across a deep blue jewel. Kṛṣṇa usually wears a yellow and Rādhā a red garment, and sometimes after a meeting they go home in each other's dress.

Kṛṣṇa is a very comely person, but the poet expends his greatest effort in depicting the perfection of Rādhā's appearance. He uses characteristic devices to this end. Rādhā has particularly beautiful eyes, ornamented with collyrium, which dart and dance like *khaṁj* birds and sometimes launch glances that can be compared to arrows flying from the bow. Her hair is usually coiffed in a style which is modeled on the moon, and her hair is so long that it has to be braided and piled at the back of her head.

The part of her hair is streaked with brilliant vermillion in token of her married state, and she wears the ornamental mark, the *tilak,* on her forehead. Her nose is pierced at the side for a pearl jewel or a golden stud, and she wears a large earring that comes down over her cheek.

She has a dark beauty spot in the middle of her chin, and her well-shaped breasts press tightly against the cloth of her bodice. Her waist is girdled with a belt of tiny bells and her feet with anklets. Her navel, which is deep and thought-provoking, is bared; her waist is thin and her hips wide. Her teeth are very white and enhanced by a cosmetic darkening of the spaces between. The soles of her feet are dyed red with henna and her toes have ornaments. When she walks, she displays the gait of a female elephant. On her arms are bangles that shimmer like light on water. The dances she performs resemble country dances, as when she is "doing steps in the *tattāthei* movement," but at the same time, "The faultless Daughter of Vṛṣbhānu/ Portrayed the various parts/ of the sudhaṁg dance./ Her technique was expert." Even if the setting of her arts is bucolic, she brings to them a mysterious air of sophistication, as of someone well-versed.

Obviously Rādhā is not a simple peasant girl, but a *nāgarī,* a city lady, one with special training in adornment and theatrical art, one who could be compared with an actress or dancing girl. To Harivaṁś these attributes, stylized and based on traditional canons, were useful aids in imagining Rādhā incarnate.

Vijayendra Snātak records twenty-four commentaries written on the *Caurāsī Pad.*[38]

In *Sphuṭvānī,* Harivaṁś' second poetic work in *Braj Bhāṣā,* one finds a miscellaneous collection of verses. Their subjects include theological discussion, the meaning of single-minded devotion, doctrinal preaching, descriptions of Kṛṣṇa's birth and of Rādhā's beauty, evocations of the bower sport, and exhortations on the service of Gopāla. Five commentaries have been written on this short anthology.[39]

Poetic Style in the *Caurāsī Pad*

Both Keay and Snātak agree that Harivaṁś was a great master of *Braj Bhāṣā,* to which he adapted a highly Sanskritic poetic vocabulary, and that his *Braj* writing excels his composition in Sanskrit. The union of *Braj* and Sanskrit in his writing gives a richness to it that surpasses the writing of Sūrdās and allows Harivaṁś to rival the great and influential master Jayadeva. He was also indebted to the poet Vidyāpati. Harivaṁś combines economy of language with a nearly perfect ability to convey, sweetly and clearly, precisely what is required for the poetic expression. In a more technical sense his manipulation of sound effects, breadth of vocabulary, and use of figures of speech is very subtle—the work of an artist with remarkable mastery of nearly every aspect of his medium.

Although Harivaṁś was conversant with and used the different forms of classical meter in his other works, in the *Caurāsī Pad* he relied exclusively on the *pad* form, which has a free-flowing rhythm, meant to be used in song. This close relationship of poetry to song is shown in the way that the *padas* are grouped according to appropriate *ragas*. This system is as follows:

1. *pad* 1–6 *Rāg—Vibhās*
2. *pad* 6–13 *Rāg—Bilābal*
3. *pad* 14–19 *Rāg—Ṭoḍī*
4. *pad* 20–26 *Rāg—Ghanāśrī*
5. *pad* 27–28 *Rāg—Vasant*
6. *pad* 29–35 *Rāg—Devagāṁdhār*
7. *pad* 36–51 *Rāg—Sāraṁg*
8. *pad* 52–56 *Rāg—Malār*
9. *pad* 57–62 *Rāg—Gaurī*
10. *pad* 63–65 *Chand—Cārī*
11. *pad* 66–71 *Rāg—Kalyāṇ*
12. *pad* 72–80 *Rāg—Kānharau*
13. *pad* 81–84 *Rāg—Kedārau*[40]

Because of the style of the *pad,* one should not think that subtle metrical effects are absent; rather, the attempt is made to provide shifting points of emphasis or of stress through meter, alliteration, and vocabulary. Unlike strict metrical form—determined in Hindi verse by syllabic length and the relation between syllables of different length—the *pad* lets the poet concern himself with meaning, emphasis, and the requirements of song, and adapt these ends to a more flexible metrical base.

An analysis of the language of the *Caurāsī Pad* is outside the scope of this study, although I shall attempt to set forth some of the language conventions used by the poet. The poet's grasp both of Sanskrit and *Braj Bhāṣā* is evident in his vocabulary, which is a rich mixture of *tatsama śabda,* Sanskrit words used in their original forms; *tadbhava śabda,* Sanskrit words adapted to the structure of Hindi parts of speech; and *Braj Bhāṣā*.[41]

Harivaṁś is skillful in the art of *anuprāsa,* consonantal alliteration. The rule for alliteration is that the same consonant must be repeated at least once and in the same order in closely following words, although letters in the same *varga* of the alphabet (aspirated, nasal, etc.) may be used alliteratively with each other.[42]

Some examples are:

Kaṁkan kiṁkini dhuni (*pad* 69, line 9)
Kiraci kiraci kuṁcukī (*pad* 70, line 6)
Surat juddh jay jut (*pad* 3, line 2)
Kal gān karat man harat (*pad* 5, line 10)
Man rahat śravan suni (*pad* 13, line 6)
Juvati calati gajagati arujhātī (*pad* 15, line 8)
Samān naiṁ aṁjan jut (*pad* 45, line 5)

The poetry is full of similar alliterative combinations which, besides lending beauty to the sounds of contiguous words, tighten the inner structure of the poetic line. Harivaṁś also used rhyme *(tuk),*[44] an invariable feature of all kinds of medieval Hindi verse. In the *pad* of Harivaṁś the end rhymes are sometimes irregular. The traditional types are (1) *sarvāntya:*[45] all lines end in the same *tuk (a a a a);* (2) *samāntya:* even numbered lines end the same (- b - b); (3) *viṣamāntya:* odd numbered lines end the same (a - a -); (4) *viṣamāntya-samāntya:* odd numbered lines rhyme and even numbered lines rhyme (a b a b); and (5) *sama-viṣamāntya:* rhyming couplets (a a b b).

The majority of Harivaṁś *pad* follow the rhyme scheme (a a a a) with these variants: *sama-viṣamāntya* (*pad* 19, 27, 30, 32, 52, 53, 57, 66); anomalous (a a b a) followed by *sama-viṣamāntya (pad* 69); *sama-viṣamāntya* (a a) followed by *sarvāntya* (*pad* 72). Only ten *pad* show the major change, the substitution of *sama-viṣamāntya* in the end rhyme for *sarvāntya.* However, the reader will notice half rhymes and partial alliterations in half-line endings to give further resonance to the music of the stanzas.

In Sanskrit prosody, upon which Hindi versification is based, the general term for poetic effect in language is *alaṁkāra,* or adornment. *Alaṁkāra* applies to the measures undertaken by the poet to skillfully use language to evoke the appropriate emotion, the *rasa,* in the reader or listener. Śrī Hit Harivaṁś is accomplished in the use of *alaṁkāra,* but Western students will need a little patience to examine ways this skill is employed in the Hindi version of the *Caurāsī Pad* so that they will notice these devices in the English translation.

First I shall try to illustrate how the poet uses recognized figures of speech to create images. An *alaṁkāra* does not merely fulfill a rule, but must be strikingly beautiful in all aspects of its expression, including sound and meter, in order to be effective. For full appreciation, the context in which a particular figure of speech is used must be examined. The following examples provide only a point of discussion. The technical terms for the figures of speech have been rendered in English to help the reader understand their applied meanings. Parenthetical numbers following each excerpt refer to *pad* and line in the *Braj Bhāṣā* text.

1. *Upamā*—simile. A comparison of the lower to the higher.[46]

Śrīphal uraj kaṁcan sī deho
Kaṭi kehari . . .

Her breasts are like śrīphal fruit:
Her body like gold—her waist like a lion's.

(43. 4, 5)

2. *Utprekṣa*—a comparison with *mano (manau),* meaning "as if" or "as though," which is more qualified in its force than *upamā.*

Aṁs aṁs bāhu dai, kiśor jor rūp rāsi
Manau tamāl arujhi rahī saras kanak beli.

The exquisite young couple
Placed arms on each other's shoulders:
It seems [as if it were] a lovely golden creeper
entwined with a tamal tree.

(17. 2, 3)

Kuc yug par nakh rekh pragaṭ mānauṁ śaṁkar śir śaśi ṭol

On both your breasts are vivid scratches
[as if they were] Like the moon-shaped mark
On Śiva's head.

(23. 5)

3. *Rūpak*—metaphor.

Bhṛkuṭi kām kodaṁḍ naiṁn sar kañjal rekh anī

Her eyebrows are [like] Kāmadeva's bows:
Her eyes the arrows,
The lines of collyrium the points.

(29. 6)

4. *Dṛṣṭānt*—it is as though the lower should be the higher.

Prīti na kāhu kī kāni vicārai
Mārg apamārg vithakit man ko anusarat nivārai.
Jyoṁ saritā sāvan jal umagat sanmukh sindhu sidhārai
Jyoṁ nādhi man diye kuraṁgani pragaṭ pāradhī mārai.
Jai śrī hit harivaṁś hilag sāraṁg jyoṁ salabh sarīrahi jārai
Nāik nipun naval mohan binu kaun apanapau hārai.

Love knows no limits.

Who can prevent
The tired mind from following
Good or evil paths?

As the river waters flood
In the month of Śrāvan
And flow toward the sea,

As the hunter kills the deer
That have openly given their minds
To the flute's sound,

Śrī Hit Harivaṁś says,
So the moth joyfully offers its body,
Burning in the lamp.

Without the wise hero,
Young Mohan,
Who can abandon himself?

(42)

5. *Pratīpa*—comparison of the higher to the lower.

Dasanani kuṁd kalī chavi lajjit

The jasmine buds are shamed
Because of the beauty of his teeth.

(64. 6)

6. *Vībhāvanā*—contradiction.

Rūp rucir aṁg aṁg mādhurī, binu
bhūṣan bhūṣit braj gorī

She has a lustrous appearance and sweetness
in all her limbs.
Even without ornaments
The Fair One of Braj is adorned.

(82. 4, 5)

7. *Vyatireka*—the lower is shown more favorably than the higher and to the detriment of the higher.

Naiṁnani par vāraum̐ koṭika khaṁjan

For your eyes I would sacrifice crores of
khaṁjan birds.

(22. 1)

Khaṁjan mīn mṛgaj mad meṭat kahā kahauṁ
naiṁnan kī bātaiṁ

What shall I say about the eyes
That efface the pride
Of the fawn, the fish and the khaṁjan bird?

(73. 1)

8. *Bhrama*—seeing one thing and thinking another.

Vaṁsī bisikh, vyāl mālā vali paṁcānan pik kīr
Malayaj garal hutāsan mārut sākhāmṛgaripu cīr

His flute has become an arrow:
The strands of his garlands, serpents,
The cuckoos and parrots, lions.

The sandal tree has become poison:
The wind, fire,
His clothes, thorny creepers.

(37. 5, 6)

9. *Viṣama*—contradiction of the normal customs or the natural state of affairs.

Jāhi biraṁci umāpati nāye,
Tāpai taiṁ ban phūl bināye

You have caused the One
To whom Brahmā and Umā's husband bowed
To pick a forest flower.

(18. 5, 6)

10. *Parivṛtti*—exchange.

Mokoṁ tau bhāvatī ṭhaur pyāre ke naiṁnani meṁ
pyārau bhayo cāhai mere naiṁnani ke tāre

To me more dear even than body,
Mind and life, the Beloved would give up
Crores of his lives for me.

(1. 3, 4)

The second aspect of *alaṁkāra* deals with the emotion and action of the heroine and hero, here Rādhā and Kṛṣṇa—for *bhakti* poetry this aspect has been distantly derived from dramatic presentation—and how these are perceived by the spectator or devotee. In the case of *śṛṇgāra bhakti* the devotee plays the role of *āśraya,* the spectator, and his feelings and actions, the *anubhāva,* are dependent upon those of the chosen deity. For Śrī Hit Harivaṁś, Rādhā becomes the *ālaṁbana,* or the object, and her actions are *uddīpana*. *Śṛṇgāra rasa* is called *rasrājā* because it contains within itself the thirty-three varieties of *vyabhicārībhāva,* whereas other *rasas* are deficient. In the framework of the *śṛṇgāra* "scenario," the actors themselves affect each other as the *āśraya* and the *ālaṁbana,* and exchange the functions of *vibhāva* and *anubhāva*. For example, in the Rādhāvallabha view of *śṛṇgāra,* Kṛṣṇa is the *āśraya* of Rādhā who is the *ālaṁbana* for him on many occasions. The *sakhīs* appear to be as *āśraya* with respect to both the divine lovers. For the human *bhakta,* although his principal devotion is to Rādhā, the various elements of the "scenario"—Rādhā, Kṛṣṇa, the *sakhīs,* Vṛndāvan, and the Jamunā River—evoke the *rasa* through their *uddīpana* and are thus capable of being *ālaṁbana* for him.[47]

The *uddīpana* and indirectly the *vyabhicārībhāva,* which form the vehicle of *rasa,* have been divided into various groups. According to Hindi theorists there are three divisions of *uddīpana: bhāva,* first impressions and reactions, sometimes called *ayatnaja* or involuntary, with no connivance on the part of the *ālaṁbana* (either *nāyaka* or *nāyikā*); *hāva,* reactions that tend to make the *bhāva* clearer or more vivid, sometimes called *yatnaja* or voluntary; and finally, *hela,* which express the feelings of the *ālaṁbana* very clearly.[48]

The *bhāva* consist in seven states: (1) *śobha,* beauty; (2) *kānti,* luster or splendor; (3) *dīpti,* light or luster; (4) *mādhurya,* sweetness; (5) *pragalbhatā,* fearlessness, intrepidity; (6) *audārya,* munificence of liberality; (7) *dhairya,* gravity or composure. However, it is in the *hāva* and *hela* that the arts of love and other human behaviors give scope to the poet's repertoire. The following are examples of *hāva* from the *Caurāsī Pad:*

1. *Vicchitti*—adorning the body.

Pratham majjan cāru, cīr kajjal tilak
Śravan kuṁḍal, vadan caṁdranī lajāvai
Balay kaṁkan cāru, urasi rājat hāru
Kaṭiv kiṁkini, caran nūpur bajāvai

Bathing first, she robes in a beautiful garment:
Putting on collyrium and tilak and earrings
in her ears.
Her face shames the moon.

. . . .

Bracelets and bangles—an elegant necklace
glitters at her breast.
A belt of tiny bells rings at her waist,
Anklets at her feet.

(81. 4, 5, 8, 9)

2. *Vivvoka*—although one likes a certain thing, one expresses oneself as though one does not like it.

Piy citvat tab candravadan tan,
Tū adh mukh nij caraṇ nihārat

Ve mṛdu cibuk praloy prabodhat
Tū bhāmini kar sauṁ kar ṭārat

When the Beloved looks at your moon-like face,
You stare at your own foot
With countenance cast down!

Tickling your sweet chin, he coaxes you—
But you, O Passionate Lady,
Push aside his hand with your hand!

(75. 5–8)

3. *Kilakiṁcita*—a very exaggerated state of joy, sometimes, but not always, marked by inappropriateness in expression.

Rahasi rahasi mohan piy ke saṁg rī
Laḍaiti ati ras laṭkat
Saras sudhaṁg aṁg meṁ nāgari
Theī theī kahat avani pad paṭkat

In solitude with Mohan, the Beloved,
The Darling is swaying
With excess of rasa.

In the movements of the excellent sudhaṁg dance
Saying—theī, theī—the Clever Lady
Stamps her feet upon the earth.

(79. 1–4)

4. *Kuṭṭamita*—indicating negative feelings externally, but having positive feelings inwardly.

Mohan man mathat mar parsat kuc nīvi hār
Vepathayut neti neti badati Bhāminī

Mohan, his mind in torment with sexual desire,
Touches her nipple, waistcloth and necklace.
The woman, throbbing, says, No! No!

(11. 9–10)

5. *Vibhrama*—appearing with clothing and ornaments disarrayed.

Rucir tilak leś kirat kusum keś
Śir sīmaṁt bhūṣit mānauṁ taiṁ na

Your beautiful tilak has become very small.
The flowers are scattered in your hair as though
You had not adorned the hair-part on your head.

(4. 5, 6)

6. *Lalita*—accentuating the desirability of the body.

Kacasaṁjaman byāj bhuj darsati musikan badan vikās

Pretending to arrange her hair,
She shows off her arms—
And her face with a smile in blossom!

(53. 5)

7. *Līlā*—imitating the action of the Beloved to call him to mind.

8. *Vilās*—when he is absent, actions that arise from thinking of the Beloved's former actions: going to where he sat, searching for his traces, such as a footprint.

9. *Moṭṭiyata*—enthusiasm for stories about the Beloved's actions.

10. *Vihṛta*—usually only for the *nāyikā* who is too shy to express her feelings.

Because they are more appropriate to prolonged *viraha, hāva* 7, 8, and 9 are not found in Harivaṁś' poems on *nityāvihāra*. The last one (10) is inappropriate to Rādhā, who is the commanding person in the relationship with Kṛṣṇa.

In the realm of *hela* the action is much more sharply etched for the spectator. For example:

1. *Mada*—intoxication.

Apnī bāt mosauṁ kahi rī bhāminī,
Auṁgī mauṁgī rahati garav kī mātī

O Lady, tell me about your affairs!
Drunk with pride,
You remain still and quiet.

(15. 1, 2)

2. *Mugdhatā*—complete astonishment or absorption.

Jai śrī hit harivaṁś āju tṛṅ ṭūṭat hauṁ bali viśad vihār

Śrī Hit Harivaṁś says,
Today all limits are breached:
I offer myself as sacrifice in their
immaculate retreat.

(32. 8)

3. *Keli*—love play.

Āju nikuṁj maṁju meṁ khelat,
naval kiśor navīn kiśorī

The fresh Youth and the young Maiden
Are sporting today
In the beautiful new bower.

(7. 1)

Other types of *hela* include *tapan,* growing thin because of separation; *vikṣepa,* feeling of separation; *kutuhala,* too much joy; *hasita,* laughing; and *cakita,* expressing joy or curiosity eagerly.

Another analytical perspective on Hindi poetry attempts to elucidate the way that the poet conveys his intended meaning. In all kinds of poetry one has to evaluate the skill with which the poet expresses his intended meaning. One cannot have beautiful poetry if the meaning itself is not conveyed in a novel, vivid, or subtle manner. Figures of speech and other *alaṁkāras* contribute to the technique of this aspect of poetry. Classical criticism provides special terminology for *lākṣana,* the quality of the writing, and *dhvani,* its underlying meaning.[49] Examples of these are the following:

1. *Sāropā*—incorporation of the quality of the thing compared or posited with the thing itself.

Pyārau bhayo cāhai mere naiṁnnani ke tāre

The beloved wants
to be in the pupils of my eyes.

(1. 4)

Expressing through *sāropā* that the Beloved wants to be "inward" to the "thing itself," namely Rādhā's eyes, is another way of saying that he wants to be totally absorbed in Rādhā: hence, this is incorporation of the thing posited with the thing itself.

Rādhe dekhi ban kī bāt

O Rādhā, look at the *Rāsa Līlā* in the forest.

(28. 1)

The literal meaning of this passage is, "O Rādhā, look at the forest affair or topic." This refers to the *rāsa līlā,* which has been posited in the novel expression *ban kī bāt.* By incorporation the poet conveys that the *rāsa līlā* is essentially a matter to be undertaken in the forest.

2. *Vyaṁgya*—similar to *sāropā;* nevertheless, this category places emphasis upon indirect statement *(dhvani),* as in line 6 of *pad* 29, used previously as an example of *rūpak:*

Bhṛkuṭi kām kodaṁḍ naiṁn sar kañjal rekh anī

Her eyebrows are [like] Kāmadeva's bows:
Her eyes the arrows,
The lines of collyrium the points.

This might be translated literally:

Kāmadeva bow eyebrow(s)
Eye arrow(s)
Collyrium line point(s)

One has to understand in these condensed images that the poet is speaking metaphorically of the beauty of Rādhā's eyes and eyebrows; moreover, that these eyes and eyebrows can wound one with shafts bearing love's poison, as do the arrows of Kāmadeva.

The whole of *pad* 14 is more indirect. Its intention is nearly unintelligible without special information as to its meaning. The following are samples:

Adhar aruṁ tere kaise kai durāuṁ
Ravi śaśi śaṁk bhajan kiyau apvas
Adbhut raṁgani kusum banāuṁ

How shall I conceal the redness of your lips?

Try to control those traits of sun and moon—
Then I shall adorn you
With kusum flowers of rare hues.

(14. 1-3)

The reader must know that Kṛṣṇa is being addressed by one of the *sahacārīs* and that the context of the address is the situation arising when Rādhā goes to the bath and Kṛṣṇa is left alone. In *nityāvihāra* terms he suffers *viraha* only briefly, but nevertheless intolerably. The *sakhī* is analyzing Kṛṣṇa's qualities to see whether she can disguise him as a woman so that he can enter the bath and be with Rādhā. The *sakhī* goes through his traits, and finds the redness of lips is a problem. "The traits of sun and moon" refer to separation and meeting or union; thus Kṛṣṇa will be downcast when he enters the bath until he sees Rādhā. The joy he expresses then will lead her to suspect that he has entered among her attendants in disguise. Other lines of *pad* 14 are similarly obscure. As one can see, it is correct to speak also of this aspect of the analysis of poetry as its *dhvani,* or underlying meaning. The art of poetry is to draw the reader or listener to understand at deeper levels than the literal.

In concluding this discussion of poetic style, we may say that the use of metrical devices and the various kinds of *alaṁkāras,* together with the flexible form of the *pad;* the brilliance and originality of the language;

the subtle interaction of words and meaning; the subject matter, a kind of scenario, treating the amorous meeting of the attractive Rādhā and Kṛṣṇa; the music, of the language and of the song form, meant to be presented with instrumental accompaniment; and the cultic setting of the poetry's use: all these elements must be kept in mind to fully appreciate the effect Śrī Hit Harivaṁś has aspired to in the *Caurāsī Pad*.

NOTES

1. R. T. H. Griffith, *The Hymns of the Ṛgveda* (Varanasi: Chowkhamba Sanskrit Series Office, 1963), p. 64.
2. Vijayendra Snātak, *Rādhāvallabha Sampradāy-Siddhānt Aur Sāhitya* (New Delhi: National Publishing House, 1968), p. 165. Dr. Bhagabat Kumar Goswami, in *The Bhakti Cult in Ancient India,* 2d ed. (Varanasi: Chowkhamba Sanskrit Series Office, 1965), p. 105: "In numerous hymns of the *Rigveda, Rādhās* or *Rādhā* is clearly synonymous with *irā,* wealth or plenty of food. Although worshippers approached almost every god for food, and food therefore might be supposed to belong to every one of the gods, it belonged, in truth and reality, to *Indra.* He is *Satyarādhas* and none else . . . . *Rādhas* is His (*tava rādhaḥ somapītāya* [sic] *Rig Veda* 1. 51) [transcription not in original] and he gives it as the most prized treasure (*dātā rādhaḥ stuvate kāmāṁ* [sic] *vasu* [*Rig Veda* 2. 22. 3c]). He is the lord of *Rādhās* (*stotraṁ rādhānāṁ pate girvāho vīr . . . Rig Veda* 1. 30. 5a). Thus *Rādhā* was only another aspect of *Śrī.* She was rather the fountain head of real splendour and fortune (*sunṛtā vibhūtiḥ* [sic]). No wonder that she should ultimately come out as the most favourite partner of life of the Great One, when He manifested Himself as an embodiment of reality in all its glorious magnificence, for who else but *Rādhā* as the incarnation of the principle of highest splendour could legitimately claim to be by His side?"
3. S. B. Gosvāmī, *Kṛṣṇa Bhakti Kāvya Meṁ Sakhī Bhāva* (Banaras: Chowkhamba Vidhyabhavan, 1966), pp. 229, 240; S. B. Das Gupta, *Śrī Rādhā kā Krama Vikāsa* (Banaras: Hindī Pracārak Pustakālya, 1956), pp. 3–115.
4. Dhirendra Varma, *Hindī Sāhitya,* II (Prayāg: Bhāratīya Hindī Pariṣad, 1959), p. 344. Snātak, *Rādhāvallabha Sampradāy,* p. 177.
5. Rūpanārāyaṇa, *Brajbhāṣā ke Kṛṣṇakāvya meṁ Mādhurya Bhakti* (Delhi: Youngman and Co., 1962), pp. 52–55; S. B. Das Gupta, *Śrī Rādhā kā Krama Vikāsa,* pp. 115–139; D. Varma, *Hindī Sāhitya,* pp. 336–341; Snātak, *Rādhāvallabha Sampradāy,* pp. 173 ff. *Gāthāsapthaśati:* Kṛṣṇa by rubbing his face against Rādhā's face humbles the pride of the *gopīs; Veṇīsaṁhāra* of Bhaṭṭanārāyana (eighth century C.E.); *Dhvanyāloka* of Ānandavardhana; *Kavīndrasamuccaya* (tenth century C.E.); *Nala Campū* of Trivikrama Bhaṭṭa (tenth century C.E.); *Sarasvatīkaṇṭhabhāraṇa* of Bhojarājā (eleventh century C.E.); *Prākṛtavyākaraṇa* of Hemacandra (twelfth century C.E.); *Daśarūpaka* of Dhanaṁjaya; *Rāmārādhā* of Sāradātānaya (twelfth century C.E.); *Kṛṣṇa Karṇāmṛta* of Līlaśuka and *Śrī Kṛṣṇa Līlāmṛta* of Iśvarapuri.
6. Edward Balfour, *The Cyclopaedia of India,* 3d ed. (London: B. Quaritch, 1885), p. 335. "Rādhā, the celebrated mistress of Kṛṣṇa, was the wife of Angīra Goṣa, a cowherd of Gokul, with whom she lived within a forest near the Jamunā; she was one of Kṛṣṇa's favorite mistresses, the chief of the gopīs, the nymphs of Vraja";

J. Dowson, *A Classical Dictionary of Hindu Mythology and Religion* (London: K. Paul, Trench, Trubner & Co., 1903), p. 251; W. J. Wilkins, *Hindu Mythology, Vedic and Puranika* (London: Thacker, Spink & Co., 1913), p. 214; John Garrett, *A Classical Dictionary of India* (Madras: Higginbotham & Co., 1871), p. 495. She is also the most anthropomorphic of the goddesses associated with Viṣṇu or Kṛṣṇa. Kṛṣṇa has Lakṣmī in Vaikuṇṭh (Viṣṇu's heaven) with four hands and Rādhā with two hands in Goloka; S. S. Citrāna, *Bhāratvarṣīya Prācīna Caritra Koṣa* (Poona: Bharatīya Caritrakoś Maṇḍal, 1964), p. 723.

7. Dhirendra Varma, *Hindī Sāhitya,* p. 33.
8. S. B. Das Gupta, *Obscure Religious Cults* (Calcutta: University of Calcutta, 1962), p. 125. "Srī Caitānya placed himself in the position of Rādhā and longed with all the tormenting pangs of heart for union with his beloved Kṛṣṇa; but the Vaiṣṇava poets, headed by Jayadeva, Caṇḍidās, and Vidyāpati, placed themselves rather in the position of the Sakhīs, or the female companions of Rādhā and Kṛṣṇa, but ever longed for the opportunity of witnessing from a distance the eternal love making of Rādhā and Kṛṣṇa in the supranatural land of Vṛndāvana (aprakṛta Vṛdāvana)."
9. Viśvanath Prasad Miṣra, *Hindī Sāhityā kā Atitā* (Banaras: Vārīvitāna Prakāśan, 1964), part I, p. 194.
10. Charles S. J. White, "Kṛṣṇa as Divine Child," *History of Religions* 10, no. 2 (November 1970).
11. N. Shukla, *Le Karṇānanda de Kṛṣṇadāsa* (Pondichéry: Institut français d'indologie, 1971), pp. 14–17.
12. Jayanath Nalin, *Bhakti Kāvya meṃ Mādhurya Bhāva kā Svarūpa* (Delhi: Bansal & Co., 1966), p. 39.
13. Snātak, *Rādhāvallabha Sampradāy,* p. 166.
14. S. B. Das Gupta, *Śrī Rādhā kā Kramavikāsa,* p. 284. S. B. Goswami, *Kṛṣṇa Bhakti,* pp. 254–255.
15. Snātak, *Rādhāvallabha Sampradāy,* p. 168, quotes Barth, *The Hindu Religions of India,* p. 236.
16. S. B. Das Gupta, *Śrī Rādhā kā Kramavikāsa,* pp. 139–141. Also Snātak, *Rādhāvallabha Sampradāy,* p. 176.
17. S. B. Das Gupta, *Śrī Rādhā kā Kramavikāsa,* p. 178. Rūpanārāyaṇa, *Brajbhāṣā ke Kṛṣṇakāvya,* p. 62.
18. A part of this material is derived from Lalitācaraṇ Gosvāmī, ed., *Śrī Hit Caurāsī* (Delhi: National Publishing House, 1963), pp. 15 ff.
19. Snātak, *Rādhāvallabha Sampradāy,* pp. 199–205.
20. *Ibid.,* pp. 206–209.
21. *Ibid.,* pp. 210–214.
22. *Ibid.,* pp. 214–221. Although it is not mentioned among the main elements of the *nityavihāra* by the contemporary leaders quoted above, it is obvious that the Jamunā River is a contributing element, a backdrop for the scenario as the gentle, sweet-smelling breeze is cooled, blowing across its glistening surface. At other times the river seems almost to be a living being, nearly one of the *sahacārīs,* delighting with the others in the amorous ecstasy. See N. Shukla, *Le Karṇānanda,* p. 52.
23. Shukla, *Le Karṇānanda,* p. 179.
24. Snātak, *Rādhāvallabha Sampradāy,* p. 224.
25. *Ibid.,* p. 228.

26. *Ibid.*, p. 236. The closest religious movement, structurally, to the Rādhāvallabha Sampradāy might actually be the Sūfī, particularly in those areas in which the literary model of the Persian *masnavi* prevailed. According to that genre, the seeker after union with God conceived of the goal under the guise of a supremely beautiful, transcendently perfect woman. This was not to say that God (Allah) was thought to be a woman; yet, in the devotional mode, it is only natural that erotic union with the divine must sometimes involve the symbolic interplay of male and female. Since, apart from the Rādhāvallabha and similar sects, it was among Sūfī devotees that the Supreme was symbolized as a woman, one might posit the Sūfī as stimulus for the Hindu.
27. Snātak, *Rādhāvallabha Sampradāy,* pp. 240–241.
28. *Ibid.*, pp. 241–242.
29. *Ibid.*, pp. 242–246.
30. *Ibid.*, p. 247.
31. *Ibid.*, pp. 248–249.
32. *Ibid.*, pp. 250 ff.
33. This discussion is based on Snātak, *Rādhāvallabha Sampradāy, pp. 270 ff.*
34. Growse, *Mathura,* pp. 206–207.
35. Snātak, *Rādhāvallabha Sampradāy,* pp. 282 ff.
36. See translation for full text.
37. See translation for full text.
38. Snātak, *Rādhāvallabha Sampradāy,* p. 302 ff.
39. *Ibid.*, p. 307.
40. The *pad* numbers refer to those found in the text upon which the translation is based, Śrī Lalitācaraṇ Gosvāmī, *Caurāsī Pad.*
41. Snātak, *Rādhāvallabha Sampradāy,* p. 315 ff.
42. Discussion of the various aspects of Hindi prosody is found in Rāmbahorī Shukla, *Kāvya-Pradīp* (Allahabad: Hindi-Bhavan, 1969). For *anuprāsa,* see Snātak, *Rādhāvallabha Sampradāy,* p. 107 ff.
43. See note 40.
44. R. Shukla, *Kāvya-Pradīp,* p. 288.
45. *Ibid.*, p. 289 ff.
46. *Ibid.*, p. 132 ff. For discussion of *alaṁkāras* in relation to Harivaṁś' style, see Snātak, *Rādhāvallabha Sampradāy,* p. 321 ff. The transliterated *Braj Bhāṣā* lines here and in the following examples are from the text at the end of this volume, and the translations are found hereafter.
47. See Introduction, Part I, for the basic analysis of these conventions. On the question of *anubhāva,* the reactions of the *āśraya,* we can note from R. Shukla, *Kāvya-Pradīp,* p. 53 ff., that the *anubhāva* are likewise of two kinds: *sāttvika,* involuntary and *kāyika,* voluntary. Of the former the following are mentioned: (a) *stambha,* astonishment; (b) *sveda,* perspiration; (c) *romāñca,* horripilation; (d) *svarbhānga,* changing or losing voice; (e) *kampa,* fear and trembling; (f) *vaivarnya,* change of color; (g) *aśra,* tears; and (h) *pralaya,* unconsciousness.
48. See Snātak, *Rādhāvallabha Sampradāy,* p. 310 ff; and R. Shukla, *Kāvya-Pradīp,* p. 66 ff.
49. See Snātak, *Rādhāvallabha Sampradāy,* p. 320 ff.

The Translation

The Caurāsī Pad

ONE

Whatever the Beloved does seems
Pleasant to me.[1] Whatever seems pleasant
to me the Beloved does.

A good place for me to be is
In the eyes of the Beloved. The Beloved wants
to be in the pupils of my eyes.

To me more dear even than body,
Mind and life, the Beloved would give up
Crores[2] of his lives for me.

Śrī Hit Harivaṁś[3] says, hail to the Swan
And his Mate, the dark and the fair![4]
Who, pray tell, can separate waves from water?

TWO

O Sulky Lady,[1] the Beloved has called!
How beautiful it is tonight for the meeting
Of the lightning with the fresh cloud.[2]

O Sakhī,[3] Mohan is the lord of lovers.
Who is the Passionate Lady
That could be angry with him in such a way?

Śrī Hit Harivaṁś says, hearing these words,
The Beloved, whose walk is like the elephant's,[4]
Met the one who is Rādhā's Lover.

THREE

Early in the morning, the couple eager for love
Very joyously engaged
In the victorious battle[1] of sexual delight.

Weary, her lotus face was bathed
With dense drops, and the ornaments
Were scattered on her limbs.

Her tilak[2] had nearly disappeared.
Her curls were loose and appeared
Like bees, deceived by her lotus face.

Śrī Hit Harivaṁś says, their words and eyes
Are colored with the color of love.[3]
The girdle of her silken skirt has come undone!

FOUR

O Young Maiden, today your face is filled with bliss,
Announcing the joy and happiness
Of your meeting with the Beloved.

Your words are very langorous.
Your cheeks are red
And red your two tired and sleepless eyes.

Your beautiful tilak has become very small.
The flowers are scattered in your hair as though
You had not adorned the hair-part on your head.

The Generous One, who is a treasure of mercy,
Keeps nothing back
But gives his essence when he begins to give his lips.

O Timid One,[1] why do you conceal the garment[2]
You have exchanged with the Beloved—
  overpowering[3] and instructing Śyām
In the hundredfold sports of love?

The garland has fallen down upon your breast .
The clasp of your belt of tiny bells is loosened.
Śrī Hit Harivaṁś praises that sleeping[4] in the house of creepers!

FIVE

Today early in the morning
The splendid Couple are joyously drenched in pleasure
In the temple of creepers.

That charming pair, one dark one fair,
Filled with love's color, are swaying together.
Their feet keep them on the earth.

The saffron powder of her nipples
Stains the strands of the garland
On the chest of the Lord of erotic love, Śrī Śyām.

The Beloved is adorned with the marks of love[1]
Which the Crown Jewel among wise men
Gave with his own hand.

The couple, filled with love and joy,
Sing so sweetly
That they capture each other's hearts.

Śrī Hit Harivaṁś says, the humming bee, intent upon their praise,
Lends a sweeter tone
To their song.

SIX

O Darling,[1] who is
That clever, young maiden, your sweetheart,
Whom you meet by night stealthily?

Listen, my dear,
How can this fact be kept secret through pretense?
Your eyes are moist with the color of love and pleasure.

On your breast are the moon-prints of nails.
You wear someone else's clothes.[2]
Your speech is confused.

Śrī Hit Harivaṁś says, hail to Rādhā's Lord,
Who, full of love,
Is tormented by Kāmadeva!

SEVEN

The fresh Youth and the young Maiden
Are sporting today
In the beautiful new bower.

Their mutual love
Is completely incomparable.
It is heard that this couple is unique on earth.

Where the earth is made
Of various crystals and corals[1]
And the powder of fresh camphor is abundant,

There is a sleeping couch
Made of tender young leaves
On which Śyām has caused the Fair One to sit.

The couple is wholly occupied
With their joy-filled lovemaking.
The betel juice has stained their lotus cheeks.[2]

There is a charming struggle
Of the fair and the dark hand
Over the unloosening of the waistband cord.

Having seen her own reflection
In the mirror on Hari's breast,[3] the Innocent Lady,
Deluded and distressed, became very angry.

Most agreeably stroking her chin
And explaining that it was her own reflection,
The Beloved implored her to understand.

Having heard again and again
Those nectar-filled words, No! No!
Lalitā and the others gaze[4] from where they are secretly hidden.

Śrī Hit Harivaṁś says that snatching
At the necklace with her hand
In the anger of love, she broke it.

EIGHT

Oh, your lotus eyes are very red!

Filled with the color of love,
They are slow and unnatural.
Awake the whole night—Oh, Your collyrium[1] is smeared!

Below the languid eyelids
Your pupils—darting back and forth
Pierced the deer-like Mohan so he cannot move.

Śrī Hit Harivaṁś says, O one with the charming
Walk of a swan, You confuse
Your bee-like Sakhīs![2]

NINE

The couple,
Śrī Rādhā and Mohan
Are adorned.

Śyām is as charming
As the deep blue sapphire.
The Fair One has a body of gold.

On Hari's broad forehead is a tilak.
There is a red streak painted in the midst of the moon set
Of the Passionate Lady's hair.

The Lord moves like a leader of elephants.
Vṛṣbhānu's Daughter
Has the walk of a female elephant.

The Maiden wears a blue garment.
Mohan wears a yellow garment—
On his head a red turban.

Śrī Hit Harivaṁś says,
The Lover, Rādhā's Lord,
Is dyed in the color of sensual delight.

TEN

Today the Clever Lady[1] and the Youth,
That dazzling couple are pleasing to the heart.
Oh, what shall I say about such limbs of surpassing sweetness!

In their play, placing their arms
Around each other's necks—touching cheek to cheek,
They join with the elegant circle in the Rāsa Līlā.[2]

There are the sweet sounds of flute, drum and cymbal,
Anklets and so on, the belt of tiny bells, and bangles
In Śyām and the Beautiful Lady's retreat.

Śrī Hit Harivaṁś, the Sakhī concealed, sees
The lovely movement of the sudhaṁg dance
And sacrifices her body's breath.[3]

ELEVEN

In the land of lovely and peaceful groves
Rādhā and Hari wear beautiful clothes
On a night in Śarad[1] when the moon in the heaven is full.

She has golden limbs, he is of dark blue luster:
Having met rejoicing, they are one—
As though lightning were shining in the midst of a blue jewel cloud.

He is wearing new red and yellow garments,
His love is true and without compare.
A sweet-scented, cool wind blows gently.[2]

A sleeping couch is made of tender leaves.
The Lover speaks flattering words,
But the Passionate Lady is continually adverse and angry.[3]

Mohan, his mind in torment with sexual desire,
Touches her nipple, waistcloth and necklace.
The Woman, throbbing, says, No! No!

The Lord in his beautiful play is a vehicle
For man to bear many kinds of burdens. In the love sport
Rāsa's form he is a River—The Purifier of the World!

TWELVE

O clever Rādhā, come along!
For Your sake, Śyām, the Abode of Pleasure, has brought forth
The Rāsa Līlā on the banks of the Daughter of Kaliṁda.[1]

A company of maidens dances in front of him:
They are filled with great joy at the rāga's tone.
He plays his blessed flute, the source of rasa.

Around the Vaṁśīvaṭ[2] there,
Where the earth is supremely beautiful,
The scent of sandalwood blows on the gentle air, giving ease to all.

The jasmine is budding slightly:
The forest is extremely fragrant. On the full-moon night
Of the month of Śarad the moonlight is brilliantly clear.

The Lord, the Vehicle of Salvation for men,
Gazed and filled his eyes with the Herdsman's Daughter[3]—
Beautiful from head to foot, the destroyer of amorous distress.

O Lady, enjoy his arms encircling your neck.
Bear the Ocean of Pleasure!
Śyām's love play in the new bower is worthy of the praise of the world.

THIRTEEN

—Nanda's Darling has seized my heart![1]

—I was stringing my pearls. . .
He threw pebbles and went away, O Sakhī,
Early in the morning.

Nanda's Boy,[2] foremost among lovers,
Had cast sidelong glances
On her beautiful walk.

—Oh, say, how can one keep one's senses
When the ear has heard the penetrating, sweet sound
Of Kṛṣṇa's delicious flute?

Because of Govinda's[3] moon-like face
The eyes' staring
Has become like the cakora bird's.[4]

Śrī Hit Harivaṁś says, O Sakhī,
You take the Maiden to meet the Rasa of Lovers
And offer your life to them.

FOURTEEN[1]

How shall I conceal the redness of your lips?[2]

Try to control those traits of sun and moon[3]—
Then I shall adorn you
With kusum flowers of rare hues.

The kaustubhmaṇi, tied in a beautiful silk cloth:[4]
I shall conceal your body
With lotus pollen.

Where shall I find
That to give illusion for doubts
When the gladdened moon abandons the clouds?[5]

By what trick shall I assuage
The burning of the cool moon?[6]
Water for that cannot be obtained!

Śrī Hit Harivaṁś says, O Lover of Lovers
—In your ever new love—
I shall compare the fickleness of your eyebrows to khaṁjan birds.[7]

FIFTEEN

O Lady, tell me about your affairs![1]
Drunk with pride,
You remain still and quiet.

I am exhausted talking to you:
Listen, beloved Rādhikā,[2] Shameless One!
Why don't you talk about your amorous pleasure by night?

The kusum flowers are scattered in your braid.
O listen, Doe-eyed One! Your locks are fallen
On your garment border. You speak drowsily.

Your lips are colorless:
The color has stained your cheeks.
Young Lady, you walk like a hobbled elephant!

Because of your dalliance in solitude
For pleasures with the Handsome One, your garment
And the tight red bodice over your breast have come undone.

Harivaṁś says, having heard the words of the Sakhī—
Her heart delighted,
She went smiling to her home.

SIXTEEN

Today I say depart, O Doe-eyed One![1]
The maidens in the circle dance[2] are singing charmingly,
As sweetly as excellent lady kokilas[3] when they meet their lovers.

You are very clever in the elements of sexual method[4]
And an eminent adept in the discipline
Of the movement of the dance.[5]

O young maiden, Treasure of Beauty, hear me.
The moonlit night
Is waning moment by moment!

With great excitement, says Śrī Hit Harivaṁś,
She who is the Giver of Delight in sexual love
Went to the one who is named Rādhā's Lover.

Through their kisses and caresses in solitude
Crores of dynasties of Kāmadevas[6]
Speedily became disturbed.

SEVENTEEN

Today look at the sport devised by Mohan[1] and the Braj Beauty![2]

The exquisite young couple
Placed arms on each other's shoulders:
It seems a lovely golden creeper entwined with a tamāl tree.

In the new bower the buzzing bees make a sweet sound
Full of love—the cuckoos and peacocks
Blending with it.

Their bodies, rejoicing in love, at intervals
They immerse in sexual pleasure: Harivaṁś says
His eyes are an uplifted cup, drinking moment by moment.

EIGHTEEN

O Rādhā, with beauty like a painting,
Listen to my words:
You have obtained the depthless Ocean of Rasa.[1]

You are the Daughter of Vṛṣbhān, the cowherd.
You have been embraced with joy
By darling Mohan, the Lover.

You have caused the one
To whom Brahmā and Umā's husband bowed[2]
To pick a forest flower .

You have tasted the nectar of the lips of him
Whom the Śrutis[3] called
Bliss and Not This! Not This![4]

Your beauty cannot be described.
Śrī Hit Harivaṁś says,
I sing some part of your glory.

NINETEEN

His arms placed on the Maidens' shoulders,
The Splendor of Braj, the Lover,[1]
Sports in the Rāsa Līlā.

The moon gleams in the clear sky of Śarad.
A flute of incomparable sweetness
Plays softly.

The Dark Cloud[2] is splendid:
The Braj Maiden[3] adorns him
Like the golden creeper on a tamāl tree.

Cymbals, mṛdaṁg,[4] and upaṁgā[5] play
And there are songs
That churn the hearts of crores of Kāmadevas.

In numerous ornaments and saris of varying hues
The women display the parts
Of the sudhaṁg dance.

Delighted goddesses shower kusum flowers.
In the heavens is heard
The sweet loud sound of the drums.

Śrī Hit Harivaṁś says the heart
Is immersed in the love between Śyāmā[6] and Rādhā's Lover.
It is the abode of all happiness.

TWENTY

Intoxicated with the rasa of darling Mohan,[1]

O woman, out of abashment
Why do you keep secret from me
Your first amorous experiences?

Look! You are wearing a yellow garment
Draped around yourself.
Where is your red skirt?

The string of your pearls is broken and hanging.
There are moon-shaped nail marks
On your breast.

Your biṁba-colored[2] lips are bruised.
The collyrium is smeared upon your cheeks.
Your step is faltering.

Your reddened eyes move lazily.
The kusum flowers have fallen down
In your curls.

Today in solitude Mohan
Has looted all the various treasures
In his trust.

Śrī Hit Harivaṁś says the Lady, having heard these words,
Went to her house slowly,
Smiling.

TWENTY-ONE

Your two eyes are the tale-bearers![1]

They are very lively
And uncontrolled. Somewhere you have met
The one with the bower retreat.

Your hair-part ornaments are scattered.
The kusum flowers have utterly fallen away.
Your tangled locks are swinging loose.

On your breast
The marks of nails are seen clearly.
Dear One, how can you conceal them?

The betel juice has run down
Upon your lovely cheeks.
Beautiful Maiden, your lips are colorless.

Śrī Hit Harivaṁś says,
O Rasa-bearing Lady,
Your limbs are very weak!

TWENTY-TWO

For your eyes I would sacrifice crores of khaṁjan birds.[1]

They are fickle, tremulous,
Dark red, piercing:
The forward part adorned with collyrium.

The entrancing beauty of the side glance
Of your eyes is victorious
Over hosts of Kāmadevas in the battle of sexual love.

Śrī Hit Harivaṁś says, nothing can be said
About that beauty,
Capturing the heart of the Ocean of Bliss.

TWENTY-THREE

Dear Rādhā, Your eyes are restless.

By your own love,
Golden body and youth
You purchased Manohar.[1]

Your lips are colorless.
Your curls are tangled and separated.
The betel juice has stained your cheeks.

So immersed in the joy of love,
You don't know you are wearing
A yellow garment on your body.

On both your breasts are vivid scratches:
Like the moon-shaped mark
On Śiva's head.[2]

Śrī Hit Harivaṁś says,
O Lady, you say something,
But your words are slow.

TWENTY-FOUR

Today Gopāl[1] sports in the Rāsa Līlā
At the tree of wishes[2]
On the river's bank—O Sweet Lady.

The moon is gleaming
In the clear sky of Śarad.
The threefold wind is very pleasing—O Sweet Lady.

The bakul, campak and mālati[3]
Have bloomed: joyful and intoxicated
The cuckoos and parrots—O Sweet Lady.

The countryside is pleasant
With song and sudhaṁg dance:
The crowd of Braj maidens!—O Sweet Lady.

Indra, delighted, played
Upon the tom-toms. Solemn wisemen[4]
Abandoned their austere vows—O Sweet Lady.

Śrī Hit Harivaṁś says Śyāmā's heart,
Immersed in love, dispels
The sufferings of multitudes of Kāmadevas—O Sweet Lady.

TWENTY-FIVE

Today Rādhikā, the Clever Lady, is well-adorned.

In the group of Braj maidens
She is best of all in virtue of beauty,
Modesty, lovemaking and cleverness.

A lotus is in her right hand—
Her left on a Sakhī's shoulder. Oh, she sings,
Beautifully blended with the sweet sound of the rāga!

Hit Harivaṁś says:
Informed in all knowledge, she meets in the new bower's
Solitude with the Lover, Śyām, greatly blessed.

TWENTY-SIX

Madan Gopāl's flute is enchanting.

Hearing its sweetness,
(Listen, O Rādhikā!)
Destroys the pain of the King of Desire.[2]

On the full moon night of Śarad in Vṛndā forest,
O Sakhī, a fragrant, cool wind
Was blowing very gently.

On the bank of the Chief of Purifiers[3]
The black bees worshipped the lotus.
Beneath the Tree of Wishes Balvīr[4] sported in the Rāsa Līlā.

Best in the whole circle,
You were the one who joined with Hari.[5]
To what shall I compare you, adorned in the choicest costume?

You are the one with the golden body.
Your Darling is the sapphire.
Oh, Harivaṁś is a slave for sacrifice to the two ease-giving Swans!

TWENTY-SEVEN

In the spring season Vṛndāvan is greatly blessed.
The Clever Lady glitters with ornaments.
The Fresh Youth is happy.

The white and yellow jasmine flowers, the mango blossoms
And the pollen of the sweet mādhavī creeper
Have tired out the bees.

There are campak and bakul trees
And a multitude of various kinds of lotuses.
The pollen of the ketakī and medinī has delighted Kāmadeva.

The threefold wind blows sweetly and beautifully.
The buds of the mango are half-opened.
The cuckoos and parrots sing.

On the Purifier's bank there is a dense and attractive bower
Where a sleeping couch, heaped up with pleasures,
Has been made of young leaves.

Anklets and toe rings, kettle drums, tambourines, flutes
And mṛdaṁg make their sounds as do the upaṁg, vīṇā,[1]
And the one with the beautiful mouth, the caṁg.[2]

Near the agarsat tree with colored bark
Amid red powder, saffron,
Sandalwood and musk,

The Beautiful Woman and Hari sing a charming Holī[3] song.
The birds and deer rejoice.
The river ceases flowing.[4]

Reverence, says Śrī Hit Harivaṁś,
to the meeting of the Swan and his Mate!
Let them continue in their ways and be united
In their kingdom from age to age.[5]

TWENTY-EIGHT

O Rādhā, look at the Rāsa Līlā in the forest.

In the season of vasant[1]
There are numberless half-opened kusum blossoms
And fruits and leaves.

The note of Nandlāl's[2] flute
Has called. Listen!
Why do you drowse away?

Why do you delay?
O Lady, the time
Goes vainly by!

Your Darling is handsome—
Like a sapphire. You are the one
With a golden body.

Śrī Hit Harivaṁś says,
The Couple, united,
Overwhelm each other with a host of virtues.

TWENTY-NINE

Today Śyāmā is beautiful,
The Crown Jewel
Among the group of fresh Braj maidens.

The sweetness of all her parts,
From head to foot,
Charmed Śyām, her Lord.

The plait of braided hair
Gleams
Over her golden lotus face:

It appears as though Rāhu[1]
In the midst
Devoured Her moon-set curls.

The hair-part on the Beloved's head,
Which is adorned,
Appears like good fortune's essence in a flowing stream.

Her eyebrows are like Kāmadeva's bows:
Her eyes the arrows,
The lines of collyrium the points.

Her tilak is radiant:
An earring is at her cheek,
A pearl jewel in her nose.

For her teeth like jasmine
The beautiful lips are leaves.
She gives peace to her lover's heart.

O Sakhī, in the middle of her chin
Is a very lovely,
Natural, dark spot!

Bound tightly in her bodice,
Her jewel-box breasts
Are life itself to the Beloved.

Her entrancing arms, like the stems of lotuses,
Are adorned with shimmering bangles.
Their touch can be compared to moving waters.

It appears as though the Mistress
Has made a beautiful edging
Around the tree that is Śyām's head.[2]

Her navel is as deep as a pond
For Mohan's mind,
Like a fish to play in.

Her waist is very thin.
Her hips are wide and girdled with a belt of tiny bells.
Her thighs are like the stalks of plantain trees.[3]

The brilliance of the red dye[4]—
Together with ornaments of her lotus feet
Are the protector of the Lover's heart.

Alluring him in novel ways,
The Female Elephant
Sports with the Male Elephant.

Śrī Hit Harivaṁś says,
Praise to the exceedingly spotless
Glory of Śyāmā!

Singing and hearing it
Gives pleasure:
It is the crusher of all sins.

THIRTY

Listen, O Sakhī,
The new bower
Looks very charming.

Having taken
Mādhavī and ketakī creepers,
He has adorned his house of love.

In the month of Śarad
On the night of the full moon,
A cool, gentle, fragrant breeze was blowing.

Greedy for pollen,
The bee has grown weary:
The parrots and cuckoos sing.

O Sakhī, there is a bed for the Beloved,
Made of petals and young leaves
In many different colors.

There are vessels of gold,
Filled with various sweet drinks.
They are arranged carefully on the earth.

On that bed
The skillful Boy and Girl
Amuse themselves a great deal.

The Lover's hand
Touches her beautiful breast.
She covers it over with a garment.

The Passionate Lady
Gazes with contracted eyebrows.
She is constantly contrary at every step of the way.

Agitated and very much subject
To his passion,
Hari swiftly seizes her by the shoulder.

The Clever Boy loosens
Her waistband
And pulls away her blue scarf.

The Woman
Under the pretext of anger and obstinacy
Speaks softly the sweet words, No! No!

Embracing in the reversed position,[1]
They present their beautiful and charming
Private sports.

It is as though a golden creeper
Shines on a tree
Made of sapphires.

On the surfaces of the foreheads
Of the Couple uniting
There are drops of perspiration.

Lalitā and the others
Fan with the borders of their cloaks.
The passion in their hearts is unassailable.

Śrī Hit Harivaṁś tells
As much as he knows
About the essence of the nectar of Kṛṣṇa's love.

He whose ears hear
Is the receiver of the love
Of Rādhā's tender lotus feet.

THIRTY-ONE

At dawn today
The Couple
Are very brilliant:

The Clever Lady and the Youth,
Immersed in the rasa
Of the color of sexual love.

Placing their arms
On each other's shoulders,
They gaze into each other's moon-like faces.

Intoxicated together,
They drink that rasa
With eyes as thirsty as the cakora bird's.

Her alluring, loosened locks
Are those that stole
The Darling's heart.

Embracing and kissing each other,
They sing with a slow sound—
Sweet and clear.

In the forest retreat—unsteadily stepping,
They joyously roam
Dark lanes amid beautiful bowers.

Śrī Hit Harivaṁś says,
The meeting of the two Darlings
Soothes my heart.

THIRTY-TWO

Śyām and Śyāmā today
Are sporting
In the forest.

The night of Śarad is beautiful.
Because of the moonlight
The bower shines in a lovely way.

Biting each other's lips,
They embrace.
He snatches away the cloth from her hips.

There are nail marks on their breasts—
They look with sidelong glances:
The Couple is equal in passion.

With his hand he touches
The firm breast and garland
Of the one with beautiful eyes, the Beloved.

Betel juice has run upon their clothing.
Their hair is disarrayed.
They have exhausted hundreds of Kāmadevas in the battle of sexual love.

At every instant
Their desire for sensual pleasure is extreme.
The beautiful, tender ones are very greedy.

Śrī Hit Harivaṁś says,
Today all limits are breached:
I offer myself as sacrifice in their immaculate retreat.

THIRTY-THREE

The young Couple
Shine today
In the forest.

The Son of Nanda
And the Daughter of Vṛṣbhānu
Sleepily arose at dawn.

Their footsteps fall unsteadily—
Their pace is slow.
They touch the earth with the tips of their moon-like toenails.

Their lips are bruised:
Collyrium has streaked their cheeks,
And their tilaks are small.

Even impeded by the finger-like curls,
The thieving bees—their red eyes
Cannot hide.[1]

Śrī Hit Harivaṁś says,
Because of the waves on that ocean of sensual love,
There is no restraint on the body and mind.

THIRTY-FOUR

They wander in the forest's many bowers.

They pass through
Very narrow lanes,
But do not brush with their garments.

Early in the morning,
When all have awakened from the night,
The happiness in their unsteady eyes is revealing—

Drowsy, red
And very distracted:
Some movement arises in the pupils.

Their eyebrows are playful.
Their lotus faces are gentle and charming
Because of laughter and sweet words.

The Darling,[1] very much entranced
Like a greedy bee
Was taken without cost.

Crushed, limp, black
And loosened locks of hair
Shine on their fine cheeks.

Kissing, embracing
And beautiful chin-stroking,
They unite in the reversed position.

Whenever she grows tired,
On their couch of leaves
He fans her face with his garment's fringes.

The waves of love-sport on that ocean
Drench the heart
Of the female slave, Harivaṁś.

THIRTY-FIVE

The two young people are swinging.

When they arose at dawn,
Their bodies told them
Of the color of love's delight, born in the night.

Filled with great feeling,
They sing in unison
With a low, sweet and penetrating sound.

At intervals
The eyelids of his Dear One
Charm the mind of the Beloved.

The very delicate Woman
Fears in her heart
The gusts of wind against the precious swing.

Shivering greatly,
Clasping the chest of her lover,
She offers her breasts for a new embrace.

His spotless garland
Became entangled with her bangles
And strands of his curls with her earrings.

Filled with trembling,
How shall they be disengaged?
Their bliss grew manifold.

Repeatedly gazing upon the two faces,
Like the moon and the cakora bird,
Lalitā and the others rejoiced.

Harivaṁś spreads the border of his garment:[1]
Praising
And giving his blessing!

THIRTY-SIX

Today in the forest
The beautiful Rāsa Līlā
Was performed.

On the bank
Of the pure, the auspicious Yamunā
Mohan played his flute.

Hearing the sweet sound
Of the bangles, the belt of tiny bells and the anklets,
The birds and the beasts grew joyful.

Amid the circle of young maidens
Ghana Śyām[1]
Presented a rāga[2] in the sāraṁg mode.

The blending of the cymbal, mṛdaṁg,
Upaṁg, drum and tambourine
Enhanced the ocean of rasa.[3]

The faultless Daughter of Vṛṣbhānu,
Portrayed the various parts
Of the sudhaṁg dance.

Her technique was expert.
The curls dangled in her eyes.
Her eyebrows caused Kāmadeva to dance.

She pleased the King of Braj, her Lord,[4]
By doing new steps
In the tattātheī[5] movement.

The Crown Jewel of Sovereigns,[6]
Bountiful to all,
Caused showers to fall from clouds of bliss.

As for the young maidens,
They received suitable embracing,
Kissing and fondling.

Delightedly raining kusum flowers,
The Lord of Heaven—Indra
Beat the tom-tom.

Śrī Hit Harivaṁś says, the glory of the bower
Of the Lover, Rādhā's Lord,
Has pervaded the world!

THIRTY-SEVEN

O Sulky Lady,[1]
Why don't you go
To the little house in the bower?

Without you,
Even with crores of mistresses,
The Prince suffers the pain of sexual longing.

His voice choked up,
Enduring pangs of separation[2]—agitated,
Tears flow from his eyes.

Where are you? Where are you?
O Daughter of Vṛṣbhānu!
He laments impatiently from the grove.

His flute has become an arrow:[3]
The strands of his garlands, serpents,
The cuckoos and parrots, lions.

The sandal tree has become poison:
The wind, fire,
His clothes, thorny creepers.

Śrī Hit Harivaṁś says,
The one whose heart is supremely tender
Went swiftly to her Beloved.

The one[4] who is utterly resolute—
The Great Warrior in the battle of sexual love—
Hearing this, grew frightened.

THIRTY-EIGHT

Rise and go quickly.
Why do you delay?
The Darling is calling from the bower.

Alas, Rādhā! O Rādhikā! He shouts.
Having seen the attack
Of the elephant-like Kāmadeva.[1]

The wind and the moon of Śarad
Give aid. The chest garland
Has joined the enemy.

Very frightened of the fray,
He seeks an inaccessible place:
Aren't you your Lover's Protector?

Śrī Hit Harivaṁś says,
The Braj Maiden listened
Then left very hastily,

And took and sheltered
The Fair Warrior in the battle of sexual love
Between her breast mounts.

THIRTY-NINE

The Darling wants to play the games of love.

Very carefully
With his own hand he adorned
The house in the new bower.

It is a night in Śarad.
There is a gentle,
Cool, sweet-smelling wind.

Without you, O Maiden,
Who will destroy
The distress of desire?

Why don't you go,
O one with unsteady, fawn-like eyes?
Abandon your silence now,

Śrī Hit Harivaṁś says,
O Destroyer of the Lover's distress,
Meet him!

FORTY

The Darling is seated in the house in the new bower.

The night is beautiful.
The jasmine has blossomed
In the threefold[1] wind.

You, O Sakhī, through love play
Are the dispeller of the distress of Kāmadeva
In the heart of Mohan.

O Slender-waisted One,
Why do you delay to no purpose?
What is the reason?

Hearing this,
She went swiftly:
Oblivious of her body.

Śrī Hit Harivaṁś says,
She met the one who is named Rādhā's Lover,
Greedy for rasa.

FORTY-ONE

Only one who is colored
In the color of love
Knows the mode of love.

Although the Crown Jewel
Of all the worlds
Should think himself meek,[1]

In the new bower house
On the bank of the Yamunā
The Proud Lady remains angry.

There are about him
Numberless varieties of passionate women,
Yet peace does not come to his heart.

Perishable love,
Like that of the fickle bee,
Is made from one to another .

Śrī Hit Harivaṁś says,
Only he is wise who, having abandoned all limits,
Perceives the Darling.[2]

FORTY-TWO

Love knows no limits.[1]

Who can prevent
The tired mind from following
Good or evil paths?

As the river waters flood
In the month of Śrāvan[2]
And flow toward the sea,

As the hunter kills the deer
That have openly given their minds
To the flute's sound,

Śrī Hit Harivaṁś says,
So the moth joyfully offers its body,
Burning in the lamp.

Without the wise hero,
Young Mohan,
Who can abandon himself?

FORTY-THREE

The Daughter of Vṛṣbhānu is very clever.

Listen, O messenger,[1]
Her doe eyes are capricious:
The Fair One attracts the heart of him who looks.

Her breasts are like śrīphal[2] fruit:
Her body like gold—her waist like a lion's.
Her virtues are as numerous as gusts of wind on the ocean.

Her plait is like a serpent:
Her face is equal to one hundred moons—her thighs like plantain stalks.
Her walk is stolen from the swan's.

O Harivaṁś, listen:
Tonight have my mate
Meet me in the forest.

Although the Passionate Lady is angry,
Listen—how can she whose heart
Is innocent and good remain so?

FORTY-FOUR

Come along, Pretty One!
You have been called
To Vṛndāvan.

O Passionate Lady,
Embracing his neck, why should you not look beautiful?
You are the lightning—Mohan is the new cloud.

Your bodice is red—
Your sari of various colors:
Your body is adorned with the sixteen ornamentations.[1]

All these are suitable for young Mohan.
Your śrīphal breasts and your youth
Are the gifts of union.

Secretly, her love was very great:
Śrī Hit Harivaṁś says
She went with a gladdened heart.

In the dense new bower she met
The Ocean of Rasa[2] and conquered hundreds of Kāmadevas
In the battle of sexual love.

FORTY-FIVE

Here comes the beloved Daughter of Śrī Vṛṣbhānu.

A Treasure of Beauty,
She is very much the Crown Jewel
Among the wise—and oh, her delicate limbs!

First She anointed herself and bathed,
Then she adorned her body
With a blue colored sari.

She braided her hair and traced
A beautiful tilak.
Vermillion ornamented her hair-part.

Her fawn-like eyes shone
With a line shaped
Of collyrium.

In her nose she set
A beautiful lavaṁg.[1]
She put blackening on the line of her teeth.[2]

She tied the kusum-colored bodice
Over her śrīphal breasts.
A necklace of extraordinary beauty was on top.

Her waist was thin. Her navel
Was deep in the abdomen.
Her thighs and beautiful hips were large.

The arm she placed on Śyām's shoulder
Appeared as though a lotus stem
Were made lovely with jewels.

Śrī Hit Harivaṁś says
That Couple, the Beloved and Her Lover,
Wander in the forest like a male and female elephant.

FORTY-SIX

Śyām and Śyāmā met on a night in Śarad:
In dense forest bowers with joy in the sport of love
They placed their arms on each other's shoulders.

Their hearts held great delight.
In various charming qualities the Lover and the Clever Lady
Were similar to intoxicated male and female elephants.

Because of her lovely walk, amusing blandishments, and strong desire—
By means of skill in sexual technique—the Lady, passionate for rasa,
Crushed battalions of Kāmadeva's forces.

Śrī Hit Harivaṁś says, Listen! The beauty of the Beloved
Pierced the Darling. She is very valiant,
A Fighter for the bliss of sexual dalliance.

FORTY-SEVEN

The Rāsa Līlā in the forest pleases the Darling.

In the midst of leaves and flowers
A likeness of the Beloved
From head to foot suggests itself.[1]

In confused shyness
The Greedy Bee[2] cannot embrace openly.
She runs and hides!

Creating this illusion,
In delight, the beautiful and passionate Lady
Grows excited for the strife of sexual combat.[3]

When she makes a line of collyrium in the eyes
And it appears reversed in everything,
He understands.[4]

Śrī Hit Harivaṁś says,
In the power of love's rites
Śyām calls himself Sakhī.[5]

FORTY-EIGHT

Today the Daughter of Vṛṣbhānu is bedecked.

On her body she wears various
Types of cloths and ornaments. These adornments
Are for the sake of Mohan, the Lover.

Her coquettish gestures,
Her loveliness, eyebrows and tangled locks
Despoil the pride of the other young maidens.

The sound of her ankle bells
And the ringing of her belt of tiny bells
Indicate difficult rhythmic variations.

With handsome Śyām
In the new bower
The company is very elegant.

Śrī Hit Harivaṁś says,
Joined in amorous dalliance,
Let the domain of that Couple be eternal!

FORTY-NINE

Look, O Sakhī, at the sport of Rādhā and the Beloved!

These two Young Ones
With arms around each other's neck
Dally through lanes, cattle-folds and mountain thickets.

These two adolescents
Are a treasury of beauty:
Like a golden creeper and a tamāl tree.

Biting each other's lips, kissing, embracing:
Thrilled with joy, their bodies
Grow full of the rasa of bliss.

He touches her breasts in the silken bodice:
Looking with simulated anger,
She pushes away his hand.

Śrī Hit Harivaṁś says that the Darling,
Greedy for rasa, seizes
And presses her to his chest!

FIFTY

The young Clever Girl and Clever Boy
Met and prepared a bed
Of tender lotus leaves in a bower.

The beautiful bodies of the Fair and the Dark
United on it—
As though a blue sapphire were set in pure gold.

Because of his unloosening the knot of her skirt for sexual enjoyment,
She becomes the Sulky Female toward her Lover:
A charming quarrel is stirred up in the arms of the Beloved.

Angry when his hand touches her lovely śrīphal breasts,
Pridefully the Pouting Lady cries out
And, casting sidelong glances, turns away.

Hit Harivaṁś says there was the pleasure of crores
Of sexual methods in solitude: still further,
Of those diverse and charming sweetnesses nothing was avoided!

Filled with love, the cup-like eyes of the enjoyers of rasa
(Lalitā and the others) drink that nectar.
Inwardly they lay up a treasure of happiness.

FIFTY-ONE

Pay the royal tribute, O Young Maiden!

Kṛṣṇa, the darling, clever boy is asking—
Its theft day by day
Is now clear.[1]

Your cheeks are like fresh orange blossoms,
Your teeth like a diamond line set in gold,
Your lips like lovely coral, your smile like pearl, O Fair One!

The pair of your rounded breasts are filled with nectar-like rasa.
You have a lotus face and thighs like plantain stalks
And your two eyes are like khaṁjan birds.

Everything upon you is a priceless object.
O Innocent One, why do you raise
You eyes obliquely?

Śrī Hit Harivaṁś says the sounds of the anklets and the belt of tiny bells,
The household informers,
Tell a lot!

FIFTY-TWO

See, O Sakhīs, the Pinnacle of Beauty!

The crowd of clever,
Young Braj maidens look
And bow their heads.[1]

If one could live
For crores of kalpas
And possess crores of tongues

Even then,
Nothing could be said
About the splendor of her radiant lotus face.

In heaven, earth and hell
Dynasties of poets listened
And grew afraid.

To what can the natural,
Sweet beauty of her limbs
Be compared?

Śrī Hit Harivaṁś says
In majesty, quality of beauty, and strength for his age,
Śyām is best.

Yet, daily, the Ocean of Rasa
Like a helpless creature,
Is dominated by her eyebrow play.[2]

FIFTY-THREE

O Sakhī, look at the great strength of the Weak One![1]

Mohan was like a maddened, unrestrained elephant—
Yet having looked at her,
He is bound by her curls as though they were chains.

Just now, without a struggle,
His mind's movement
Became very feeble.

But what shall I say. . .
When the Beloved looks at him
With amorous eyebrow play!

Pretending to arrange her hair,
She shows off her arms—
And her face with a smile in blossom!

Harivaṁś says, alas. . .
Because of her unusual ways at love,
Why does she cause his body such distress?

FIFTY-FOUR

New the love, new the color,
New the rasa of young Śyām
And Vṛṣbhānu's Daughter.[1]

New his yellow garment—
New her head scarf:
Very fresh the drops as the Fair One perspires.

Fresh is Vṛndāvan, verdant and charming:
Anew the cuckoos cry
And male and female peacocks.

New is the flute that plays a malār rāg
In a novel rhythm.
Hearing it, the gathered clouds came.

Their new jewels and new crowns are splendid.
They invent new steps
For the urup rhythm taken very gently.

Śrī Hit Harivaṁś's mouth gives a blessing:
Let this Couple
Be immortal in the world!

FIFTY-FIVE

Today the two lightnings met and made a wager.[1]

The very fresh black cloud
Was mediator for his love
Which filled them.

One of them, O Sakhī,
Glittered in the four directions
And looked splendid according to her nature.

The other came in for an impassioned capture:
She found her abode of bliss
Between his two arms.

Both her blue lotus eyes
And moon-like face are lovely.
The other's movement grows slow.[2]

Śrī Hit Harivaṁś says in longing for their meeting,
His heart is full
Like the moon in Śarad.

FIFTY-SIX

I offer myself as oblation to Śyām and the Clever Lady.

Night and day
Let them make their accustomed love
In the charming little house in Vṛndā forest.

The pouring forth of their laughter, amorous playfulness
And sexual dalliance restores life to Kāmadeva,
Consumed in the fire of Paśupati.[1]

Śrī Hit Harivaṁś says, O Bees[2] with fickle eyes,
Won't you make everyone blessed. . .
In a blissful place!

FIFTY-SEVEN

First of all, according to my best judgment,
I shall salute
The very delightful Śrī Vṛndāvan.[1]

Without the compassion
Of Śrī Rādhikā
It is unapproachable to the minds of all.[2]

The precious water
Of the Yamunā irrigates
Its eternal autumns and springs.[3]

The perfume of various
Kinds of flowers intoxicates
Whole clans of bees.

Cuckoos and parrots call
Amid the dark red,
Tender mango leaves.

Tribes of peacocks dance—
Tremulous
With great bliss.

The pleasure-giving wind
Blows cool and gentle
And fragrant.

Red, blue and white:
The lotuses blossom
Everywhere,

The very charming temple
In the new bower
Appears splendid.

Multitudes of loving Kāmadevas
And their attendants
Worship daily:

The Crown of Lovers,
The Couple, Śyāmā and Śyām,
Play.

Beautified by each other's arms
They arose sleepless
At dawn.

The one with the handsome,
Dark body is adorned
With a golden yellow garment.

The Passionate Lady wears a blue garment
And over her bosom
A bodice of lovely kusum color.

The cymbal, violin,
Kettledrum and tambourine play
And the sweet mṛdaṁg.

The lovely flute and the caṁg,
Which is played in the mouth,
Declare the song's beautiful rhythm.

Blending, the two sing
A Holī song
To the Gaurī Rāga.[4]

(The eyes press down
The bows of the eyebrows
And forcefully pierce the deer of the mind!)

They both clap hands
And sway,
Going to and fro.

Ho Ho Horī![5]
They cry,
Very blissful and pleasure-filled.

The Passionate Lady
Casts red powder[6]
On the Darling, her Lover.

The Beloved aims again and again
And sprinkles her from syringes,
Filled with kumkum.[7]

Sometimes they made
Resplendent swings
In the sandal trees.

Ascendent, the Two,
Swinging and thrilling,
Make merry.

The precious swing
Is shaking.
The Passionate Lady fears very much.

Thrilled again and again—
Her body trembling,
She clasps the chest of her Lover.

The hearts of her own
Well-wishing maids
Cannot contain their bliss:

Having gazed excessively with their eyes
(Their happiness having burst all bounds),
They threw themselves away!

They both are very bountiful, beautiful,
Tender and brave
In sexual dalliance.

Śrī Hit Harivaṁś says
Let those Two always act
In their everlasting retreat!

FIFTY-EIGHT

For your welfare I have come to fetch you—
Śyām has sent for you from the forest.
Dispel, O Passionate Lady, the severe distress of his desire.

Why make obstacles? Listen, O wise Rādhā!
At your meeting, O Sakhī,
Wipe out the manifest tenth stage of viraha.[1]

Look. . .Oh, the night is beautiful!
The Beloved's preparations are charming. There are lotuses
At the riverside. The Lover of Rohinī[2] is arisen in the sky.

O Sakhī,[3] You are very artful. You didn't assent
To a single one of my proposals. In speaking to you,
O Young Lady, I failed in cleverness!

Mohan Lāl is handsome.
Entranced with his own feelings:
The sweet sound of his flute enchants the birds and animals.

Śrī Hit Harivaṁś says,
O Lady, if you love Hari,
Then he will accept his body, life and youth as yours![4]

FIFTY-NINE

Who has obtained happiness[1]
By putting this mind, which is one,
In many places? Tell me!

Likewise there is trouble
Everywhere for a prostitute:
As Piṁglā[2] clearly sang.

By obstinately riding
On two violent horses
Who can run the race?[3]

Who can adopt the son
Born of a prostitute:
Tell me!

Śrī Hit Harivaṁś says,
The world is an illusion:
Everything is food for the serpent of death.

Knowing this in my heart,
I bowed my head with the worshippers
At the lotus feet of Śyām and Śyāmā.

SIXTY

What shall I say about these eyes?[1]

They are bees,
Held by the rasa of the Beloved's lotus face.
They can go nowhere else.

Whenever his curls—which are a treasure—
Cover his eyes,
He is confused and upset.

If there is the meagerest impediment to his desire—
Shorter than the twinkling of an eye—
It seems like seven hundred kalpas.[2]

There could be nothing to compare with the one who has
A lotus at her ears, collyrium around her eyes,
And musk between her breasts;

Śrī Hit Harivaṁś says,
The black-bodied one wishes to be
A fish in her pool-like navel.

SIXTY-ONE

Today, O Sakhī,
The Splendor of Braj[1] and Prabhu,[2] who is adorned,
Dance in the forest.

He has placed his arms
On the flawless shoulders
Of the young ladies.

The soft, curly locks
Of his beautifully decorated hair
Hang down on both his cheeks:

As though bees, greedy for rasa
—grown weary—
Were in the petals of the blue lotus.

He charms all hearts
By his frolicking—
He is the Destroyer of swarms of Kāmadevas!

Śrī Hit Harivaṁś says,
He makes manifest his glory
In the whole universe.

SIXTY-TWO

The Bride and Groom[1] are sporting in the Rāsa Līlā.

O Sakhī, aren't you listening
Along with Lalitā and the others ?
And looking again and again, why shouldn't your eyes be pleased?

A very melodious, sweet
And greatly enchanting sound
Is born on the bank of the Daughter of the Sun.

Repeatedly hearing the words, theī! theī![2]
That come from the mouths of the Loving Couple,
Why shouldn't you forget your body's state?

Their gentle footsteps
Raise the pollen dust of the kumkum.
Wonderful air blows from both sides.

Sometimes Śyām touches Śyāmā's
Lips, hair and breasts—
And necklace and shoulders.

Even crores of Kāmadevas cannot compare
In great beauty to their forms
And in qualities to their stylized movements.

Their eyebrow play and merriment shower bliss.
Śrī Hit Harivaṁś says,
Sway in the rasa of love!

SIXTY-THREE

Mohan Madan has three curves![1]
He enchanted
The minds of the munis.

Mohan Gopāl is full of virtues.
He is the manifestation
Of Supreme Bliss for crowds of sages.

On his head is a crown—
In his ear a jewel ring.
His chest is adorned with a forest garland.

His dark body is handsome in its yellow garment.
The lovely belt of tiny bells
At his waist is sweet.

His gem-like nails are suns.
His feet are lotuses.
He is Mohan Madan, the one with three curves.

Mohan plays His flute—
The very sound
Calls the women.

Hearing the flute's call,
The Braj women came—
Home and husband and relatives forgotten.

The darśan[2]
Of charming Madan Gopāl
Extinguished the fever of Kāmadeva.

His face filled with joy
—giving a sidelong glance—
He sings with a beautiful, sweet sound.

Śyām, who abounds in sweetness,
Places the enchanting flute
To his well-formed lips and plays.

He performed the Rāsa Līlā
In the forest in the shadow
Of the spotless Tree of Wishes.

The moon is lovely over the shore,
Near the immaculate Tree of Wishes
On a night in beautiful Śarad:

The Foster Son of Nanda sports there
As the cool, gentle,
Fragrant wind blows.

The wonderfully rhythmic mṛdaṁg
And the entrancing belt of tiny bells
Make their sounds.

The Ocean of Rasa, the Lover,
Performed the Rāsa Līlā in the forest
On the bank of the Yamunā.

Seeing his bee-like[3] play,
The birds, beasts and creepers
Are fascinated.

The deer and cows were charmed,
Along with divine maidens so immersed in love
That they threw off their garments.

Crowds of stars grew startled—
The circle moon went slow
And crores of Kāmadevas were robbed of their senses.

In very loving embraces
—Drinking from his lips—
The Sakhīs are plunged in bliss.

Śrī Hit Harivaṁś says,
Those who delight in rasa obtain their joy
In seeing his bee-like play.[4]

SIXTY-FOUR

O Sakhī, the flute is playing in Vaṁśīvaṭ.[1]

It is always springtime
In Vṛndāvan on the banks
of the holy and beautiful Yamunā.

He wears a diadem set with jewels
And an earring shaped like the makar.[2]
He has a lotus face and curls like large, black bees.

The jasmine buds are shamed
Because of the beauty of his teeth.
He is adorned with a golden yellow garment.

The one whom the munis' minds
Do not obtain in meditation
Plays games with heroic lads.[3]

Śrī Hit Harivaṁś says,
The Līlā Dancer[4] becomes manifest
For the rasa of devotees who have matchless love.

SIXTY-FIVE

Hari, who churns the mind of Kāmadeva,
Sports in a dense, new bower
On the brilliant full-moon night of Śarad.

Near the Tree of Wishes on the bank of the Yamunā
The Rāsa is performed:
O Sweet Lady, go to meet him!

The sweet mṛdaṁg plays—
All dance the sudhaṁg dance.
Haven't you heard the sound of the flute?

Śrī Hit Harivaṁś says, O Sakhī,
The Lord, the Lover of Rādhā, is precious to me—
As one who loves his devotees on earth.

SIXTY-SIX

The two lovers enjoy themselves in the bower.

In the splendor of the forest
Bursts of joy shower
Their incomparable bodies—one dark, one fair!

On Kāmadeva the Great's marvelous battlefield
The sound of ornaments
Is for the kettledrums.

As the Champions engage each other,
Crores of emotions arise
In each and every limb.

From the burden of the fighting
The Weak One is quite spent:
Her beautiful eyes drowse.

Her wearied body rests
Without care, asleep
In the Beloved's lap.

For fondling,
Her excited Lover
Touches her thighs, navel and breasts.

His body, fatigued and trembling,
He stared at that one—
Whose splendor on earth is amazing.

The Clever Lady looked up at him,
Filled with the poison of love,
And courageously gave the nectar of her lips.

Imbibing a great sweetness,
They arose quickly—
Meeting like fish in water. . .

—Just now I saw
In Your face
Such savory, biṁba-like lips!

Even though awake
His mind became entranced
And fell into the snares of hundreds of dynasties of Kāmadevas . . .

—Only once, O Beautiful One,
With a spontaneous love
Give me the nectar of your lips!

—O Sakhī, preserve
My body at the temple
Of your own Lotus Feet!

The Beloved said
—O say! Where were you, Dear One,
Great King of the new bower?

—Why this dealing
In contriving love-greedy words
Without action?[2]

Hearing such things
From the Proud Maiden's mouth,
He could not remain resolute inwardly.

His heart confused,
Pervaded by the sorrow of separation,
He heaved great sighs.

Śrī Hit Harivaṁś says,
Drawn by her arms,
He found shelter between her breasts.

The Couple's embrace
Gave birth to such joy
That the evening became a moment.

SIXTY-SEVEN

The dazzling young Bride is beautiful in the forest.

She has the sixteen beautiful ornaments
And a tilak of lotus pollen. Her eyes are fawn-like,
Her limbs perfumed, her face golden.

Her temples adorned with mahuvā flowers,
Her hair is in the moon-shape.
Her braid, bound with a vermillion cord, falls to the earth.

She attached earrings to her ears and placed a spot
On her chin. Beneath her kusum-colored bodice
The nipples of her fruit-like breasts were hidden.

Her bangles and bracelets are bright, her nails resplendent
With red jāvak dye. There are three lines in her abdomen.[1]
She wears a blue cloth and her waist is thin.

The excellent belt of tiny bells plays in the region of her hips.
A music full of sexual attraction
Plunges and raises one[2] through an ocean of rasa.

For Harivaṁś' sake the Couple,
The Crown Jewel of Lovers and the Lover of Rādhā,
Contrived various kinds of sport in solitude.

Her eyebrows conquered Kāmadeva.
With gently smiling face the Fair One
Held Ghana Śyām helpless in her love.

SIXTY-EIGHT

The Enchanter of Lovers
And the Passionate Lady
Are beautiful in the Rāsa Līlā.

During a night in Śarad,
The lovely perfume of lotuses intoxicated a multitude of bees
On the bank of the Beautiful Purifier.

Where the threefold, pleasing wind
Subdues the heat of the sun, there stands the Lover
With hundreds of passionate ladies.

To the cymbal, vīṇā and mṛdaṁg
They dance the impassioned sudhaṁg dance.
Each of them is a virtuosa at her art.

The rāgas and rāginīs, encored,
Shower nectar in the forest.
The charming flute delighted in the lips like biṁba fruit.

They sing of the beautiful, elegant one, named Rādhā,
With the seven tones[1]
In the charming Urup Rāga.

While saying—tattā theī theī—and performing new steps,
The one who moves like an intoxicated female elephant
Dances totteringly near, then back.

The New Love ran and clasped her, shining, to his breast
Where she remained. Śrī Hit Harivaṁś says,
The two are lovely swans—the Cloud and the Lightning!

SIXTY-NINE

Mohan and Mohinī[1] are well-colored
In the color of love. Intoxicated, delighted,
They dance the sweet sudhaṁg dance.

Clever in every art,
Versed in the Kalyān Rāginī,
The sweetness in their limbs is beyond description.

O Sakhī, on the bank of the Daughter of the Sun[2]
The threefold wind blows. It is as though the doves,
The cuckoos and the parrots kept the vows of munis.[3]

The Couple, The Clever Lady and the Fresh Youth,
Are beguilers of the mind. The Two sing well
With a lovely, slow and penetrating sound.

The bracelets and belt of tiny bells tinkle
When the anklets and conchs are heard:
The Fresh Young Lady showers rasa! says Śrī Hit Harivaṁś.

SEVENTY

Today, O Fair One, You are not in control.

Buffeted in the ocean of sexual union—overjoyed,
You roam
Like an intoxicated female elephant.

Enveloped in lassitude, your eyes,
Reddened and darkened with collyrium,
Show clearly your stealthy ways.

Showering on your lover
The nectar-like rasa of your compassion
Has lessened the redness of your lips.

The Young Maiden ties
A fastening to her curls
Like bees at her lotus breasts.

At their union
The bodice band was torn
And the waist cord loosened.

Watching, the young maidens,
Whose love was great,
Shower blessings.

Śrī Hit Harivaṁś says,
Let the Couple be ever permanent
In that forest on earth.

SEVENTY-ONE

Together with Śyām in the Rāsa circle Rādhikā looks beautiful.

Nandalāl is in the midst of the Braj maidens, the color
Of campak flowers, as though a cloud were surrounded
By lightning or an emerald set in gold.

The one who gives joy does the steps,
Pauses and tattā theī hand motions,
According to the seven tones, sa ri ga ma pa dha ni.

In the emotion of the dance she is a picture
In the blue costume she wears: Her face shines
Like moonlight in the cloudy skies in the sign of makar.[1]

The rāgas and rāginis and various rhythms
Adhere to musical science. The full moon rests[2]
In the heaven in a night in Śarad.

The one who moves like an intoxicated female elephant
Has dispelled the madness of Kāmadeva from the Lord,
The Swan who has the waist of a Lion, says Śrī Hit Harivaṁś.

SEVENTY-TWO

It is on the pleasure-giving, lovely and auspicious shore.

Sharing an ever new and profound
Love, the Youthful Hero
And the Clever Lady sport.

Having touched the rasa bearing
Waves of the cool Daughter of the Sun,
The breeze rains soft drops of water.

There is an excellent Tree of Wishes.
The fragrance of lotus and campak blossoms
Delights the hearts of the charming Couple.

Best in all the sudhaṁg's wantonness
They sing and dance
With voices blended in novel ways.

It astonishes crores of Kāmadevas,
Who bow their heads:
Together with fawns, peacocks, swans, bees and cuckoos.

A golden vessel, filled with sweet drink,
Shines in the grove
At the couch prepared of kusum flowers.

At evening enjoying mutually many pleasures,
The Two equip their armies
For the battle of sexual dalliance.

The Lord of troops of lovers
Seizes the hand of the young Maiden
And cleverly loosens her waistband.

No! No! She speaks her nectarine words,
But the Lover pays no heed
To the anger of love.

Śrī Hit Harivaṁś says,
The enjoyers of rasa, Lalitā and the others,
Look through an aperture in the house of creepers—

Filled to the brim with incomparable bliss,
Powerless to breathe: tears of joy
Choke their eyes and throats!

SEVENTY-THREE

What shall I say about the eyes
That efface the pride
Of the fawn, the fish and the khaṁjan bird?

Listen, O Beautiful One,
How long have you taught them
The wiles of enchantment and subjugation?

With sidelong glances, fearless, unsteady,
Penetrating, red, black and white:[1]
Whence were they created?

These eye glances,
As sweet and intoxicating as honey,
Fear not but seize everything of others.

O Passionate Lady,
Your eye didn't look at me fully
With even a little favor![2]

Śrī Hit Harivaṁś says,
O beautiful Swan-gaited Lady,
Do what you like for love!

SEVENTY-FOUR

O Fawn-eyed One,
Why do you build up
Your anger?

I am so fearful and hesitant
That I cannot say
A single thing!

Intoxicated, he sings of you
On the flute and in his heart:
Recalling your beauty awake and asleep.

Śrī Hit Harivaṁś says, you are the Destroyer of Sorrow,
Born of separation, in the one grieved with sexual desire,
The Great Lover, Mohan.

SEVENTY-FIVE

O Sakhī listen,
Why don't you agree
With a single thing that I say?

Why do you differ with your Lover
—Who is your life—
Without fault on his part?

When the Beloved looks at your moon-like face,
You stare at your own foot
With countenance cast down!

Tickling your sweet chin, he coaxes you—
But you, O Passionate Lady,
Push aside his hand with your hand!

Helpless, irresolute and very much distressed
Because of separation
He has no thought for what is appropriate or inappropriate.

Śrī Hit Harivaṁś asks,
Having met the Lover in solitude,
Why not satisfy his thirsty eyes?

SEVENTY-SIX

In the Clever Lady's bower house
The bed is made of clusters of tender leaves.
Oh, the very bountiful Maiden is expert in sexual art!

From the joy of sexual union the waves of sweetness
In her eyebrow play, amorous emotions, and limbs
Churn up crores of Kāmadevas.

In the beautiful retreat—amid sonorous anklets
And the natural and unusual sound of the belt of tiny bells—
The Lord cries, Stop! Stop!

The meeting of the Lord of Adolescents
And his Beloved (the Swan and His Mate)
Bathes Harivaṁś' eyes with excellent sweet rasa.

SEVENTY-SEVEN

Filled with delight, the Young Lady, dangling and whirling,

Had swung with her Lover in the swing of sexual love
Throughout the whole lovely night
In the house of creepers.

Although distraught
From excessive drinking of the rasa of passion,
She kept up the pace.

Her eyes enveloped in languor,
Her locks scattered:
The bodice upon her breast was slightly opened.

Her garland crushed,
The waistband loosened:
Her garment was stained with collyrium and betel juice.

Śrī Hit Harivaṁś says,
Rādhā is the herb, restoring life to tired Śyām,
Utterly pierced by the arrows of Kāmadeva.

SEVENTY-EIGHT

The Young Maiden dances the sudhaṁg dance.

Saying—theī, theī—She looks
(As though she were a thirsty, female cakora bird)
Toward the Beloved's moon-like face.

Seeing how clever she is
In uniting rhythms and pauses,
Śyām cries, ho ho rī!

Śrī Hit Harivaṁś says,
The sweetness of her limbs
Attracted Mohan's mind with force!

SEVENTY-NINE

In solitude with Mohan, the Beloved,
The Darling is swaying
With excess of rasa.

In the movements of the excellent sudhaṁg dance
Saying—theī, theī—the Clever Lady
Stamps her feet upon the earth.

The Crown Jewel of those who know the numerous
Arts of sexual love, she winks with bent
Eyebrows—according to the rules.

Being as subject as a greedy bee,
The Beloved, watching,
Snaps his fingers.

The King, the Crown Jewel among lovers
In numbers of virtues, teases
And pulls at her garment, necklace and brooch.

Śrī Hit Harivaṁś says, the women attendants nearby
Drink the liquor of that bliss
In cup-like eyes.

EIGHTY

The Gopī,[1] Who appears like a golden creeper
With Śyām, the Tamāl tree,
In all her limbs is pleasing to the heart.

Her face has the moon's brilliance. The splendor of her curls
And tilak are like its black spots. She hides herself
In Kṛṣṇa's lap as does lightning in the cloud.

Naked, she is like a golden column—
The length of her braid like a snake. Ardently,
The Passionate Lady in the bower embraces her Lover's neck.

Śrī Hit Harivaṁś says that Rādhikā
—With the beautiful name and breasts that are domes of gold—
Tired from sexual dalliance, looks beautiful with her Lord.

EIGHTY-ONE

The Daughter of Vṛṣbhānu sings sweet and melodiously.

A pleasing and variegated tone
From the carcarī rhythm inspires delight
In the Foster Son of Nanda's heart.

Bathing first, she robes in a beautiful garment:
Putting on collyrium and tilak and earrings in her ears.
Her face shames the moon.

She wears a lovely nose set
Of gold, studded with jewels.
Her lips like baṁdhūka flowers, her teeth gleam like the jasmine.

Bracelets and bangles—An elegant necklace glitters at her breast.
A belt of tiny bells rings at her waist,
Anklets at her feet.

The Passionate Lady with the swan's charming walk
Incites to love's madness. The color of henna
Gives brightness to her nails.

Her dance is an ocean of exultation—
In solitude the Clever Young Lady's moonstep
Reveals many mysteries.

Versed in the arts of sexual dalliance,
The expert beauty of her dance technique and eyebrow play
Cause Kāmadeva to dance.

In the house in the dense forest
—Having beautified the Lover with her arm—
A charming conversation rains a plenitude of bliss.

Let Harivaṁś, the bee, obtain the nectar flowing
From the lotus of erotic love
In the ocean of Their union!

EIGHTY-TWO

The Young Maiden is a treasure of cleverness.

The Dark One, the best
Among all the clever young men, is helpless—
Having turned and glanced at her face.

She has a lustrous appearance and sweetness in all her limbs.
Even without ornaments
The Fair One of Braj is adorned.

At every moment expert in the motions of the sudhaṁg dance,
Ardent in her knowledge of the sexual arts,
She plunges and rises through an ocean of rasa.

Confined at the nipples of her young breasts,
Like golden lotuses, is the unsteady and bee-like
Mind of Mohan, the Lover.

The eyes of her Beloved
Are a pair of khaṁjan birds,
Bound by various bands and cords.

It is as though some intoxicating wine were mingled
In the pool of her navel:
In that abdomen comparable to the earth.

Śrī Hit Harivaṁś says, the handsome groom,
Drinking, tore asunder
The powerful limitations of the Vedas.[1]

EIGHTY-THREE

Forsake, O Sulky Lady, the anger held in your heart!

Why do you treat the Dear One of your life like this?
He is courteous, handsome, young, virtuous
And submissive to your words.

Hari recites your holy Name helplessly
All the time. He recalls you in his heart
Without a moment's respite.

The charming night of Śarad is waning
Moment by moment. O Passionate Lady,
Be inclined toward sweet eros!

Listen and accept, O Sakhī, what I am saying
In my own words. O Lovely Faced Lady,
He tastes the heavy sorrow of separation without cause.

Hit Harivaṁś says, meeting on the couch of tender leaves
In the bower, they perform their beautiful sports
And swim in an ocean of pleasure.

EIGHTY-FOUR

Oh positively! Today the Sweet Lady appears full of pleasure.

Your sequestered rendezvous does not hide itself,
  O Daughter of Vṛṣbhānu,
From me! Your waistband was loosened when you entered
Into the battle of sexual dalliance with Nanda's Beloved Son.

The string of pearls was broken and the moon-shaped hair pulled down:
The Lover plundered you in solitude!
The betel juice has run upon your cheek.

Your eyes are full of languor, your lips like biṁba colorless.
You throb from love's caress. Śrī Hit Harivaṁś says,
Oh, you are so beautiful!

Notes to the Translation

STANZA ONE

1. "the Beloved," Kṛṣṇa; "me," Rādhā. Throughout the translation, capitalization has been used selectively to give the sense of reference to deity and not to ordinary human lovers.
2. Crore = 10,000,000.
3. It is the convention in this type of poetry for the poet to identify himself by inserting his own name into the last line of the stanza. It is conventional, also, to translate the poet's name as in the phrase, "Śrī Hit Harivaṁś says . . . ."
4. Kṛṣṇa and Rādhā respectively. Throughout the poem the divine couple are compared to swans, i.e., *haṁsa,* an Indian bird not strictly speaking a swan but one to which in English it is customary to give that name. It is considered a creature of great beauty and is also a symbol of the highest spiritual level.

STANZA TWO

1. "Sulky Lady" and "Passionate Lady" are conventional epithets for the *nāyikā,* or heroine, in Sanskrit dramaturgy. They also refer to the emotional states of women in stages of sexual play and arousal, described in the *Kāmasūtra.* In other stanzas of the poem, many different epithets are used both for Rādhā and for Kṛṣṇa.
2. "Lightning" is of golden color and hence represents Rādhā; Kṛṣṇa is frequently called the cloud, *megha,* which is a kind of pun since the word also means dark.
3. "Sakhī" means female companion or friend. Here it appears that Rādhā is being addressed in a familiar way by one of the female friends.
4. It is usual to compare a beautiful woman's walk to that of an elephant's, whose walk is indeed very graceful. Moreover, elephants in rut display great feeling and certain striking physical characteristics, an impressive spectacle and one that to the Indian poets suggested metaphors and similes relating such passion to that of humans.

STANZA THREE

1. A recurring theme is the comparison of sexual intercourse with a battle. To be sure, as outlined in the *Kāmasūtra,* it requires much biting, pinching, and scratching to complete the act. Moreover, the battleground of love is the one in which the protagonists defeat the hosts of Kāmadeva or Eros.
2. Forehead mark.
3. "Colored with the color of love," *madan raṁg raṁgi rahe.* This metaphor appears throughout and refers as much to an emotional state as to certain physical characteristics.

STANZA FOUR

1. While being addressed by the female friend, after erotic dalliance, Rādhā, as a modest girl, appears timid.
2. Either as a token of love or in blissful forgetfulness, Rādhā returning from the bower is wearing one of Kṛṣṇa's garments.
3. Again the battleground motif and a reference to Rādhā's superiority over Kṛṣṇa.
4. *Śain,* sleeping or lovemaking *(Śayan).*

STANZA FIVE

1. In Vatsyāyana's *Kāmāsūtra* eight kinds of scratching with the nails are described: (1) sounding; (2) half moon; (3) a circle; (4) a line; (5) a tiger's nail or claw; (6) a peacock's foot; (7) the jump of a hare; and (8) the leaf of a blue lotus. *Vatsyāyana's Kāmāsūtra* (Delhi: Asia Press; New Delhi: R. & K. Publishing House, 1967), p. 42.

STANZA SIX

1. In this stanza the female friend is evidently addressing Kṛṣṇa.
2. As in stanza four, line five.

STANZA SEVEN

1. This is one indication that the Vṛndāvan of faith is not wholly a site in nature but has undergone some degree of "heightening" to make it into paradise.
2. Leaves of betel, together with certain condiments, are chewed as a mild relaxant following meals and at other times in India and the East. Lovers take betel leaves in quantity as an aphrodisiac.
3. Probably the "Kaustubh" jewel or one of the ornaments with it.
4. The "friends" peeping through the vines and branches of the bower at the love sport typify the devotee.

STANZA EIGHT

1. Collyrium is a cosmetic used around the eyes.
2. The line contains a double meaning. The actual word used in *Braj Bhāṣā* is *alin,* meaning bee. The poet elsewhere used *alī,* or *āli,* for *sakhī,* which suggests bee but may also mean friend. The female friends hover around Rādhā and Kṛṣṇa like certain bees around the lotus. Here, the confusion for the "bees" lies in the fact that Rādhā has been compared to a swan and a lotus; hence, they do not know how to react!

STANZA TEN

1. The word used is *nāgarī,* a town lady or sophisticate.

2. Here and in other stanzas Rādhā participates with Kṛṣṇa in the famous circle dance, given the name *Rāsa Līlā* or the "sport of amorous ecstasy." Kṛṣṇa is a partner to all the *gopīs,* or cowmaids, simultaneously by a magical reduplication. Though it is a dance, it is regarded as the image par excellence for *śṛṅgāra rasa.*

3. Here the word *āli,* bee or *sakhī,* is used appositively with Harivaṁś, a reference to the stance of the devotees as female companions. Harivaṁś' ecstasy is so great in beholding the divine couple dancing that he gives his life as a sacrifice to them. *Sudhaṁg* may be a special type of dance, as I have construed it throughout these stanzas, or it may mean "beautifully styled."

STANZA ELEVEN

1. Autumn.
2. One of the inherent features of the divine Vṛndāvan.
3. A convention mentioned in the *Kāmasūtra.*

STANZA TWELVE

1. Jamunā.
2. The tree beneath which Kṛṣṇa stands to entice the *gopīs.*
3. Rādhā, daughter of Vṛṣbhānu, the herdsman.

STANZA THIRTEEN

1. Rādhā is speaking to the *sakhī.*
2. Kṛṣṇa is Nanda's foster son.
3. Kṛṣṇa.
4. The *cakora* is fabled to subsist on moonbeams.

STANZA FOURTEEN

1. The accepted interpretation of this stanza in the Rādhāvallabha Sampradāy was given to me by Śrī Hitjīvan Gosvāmī. Kṛṣṇa, because his passion is so great that he cannot bear to be separated from Rādhā for a moment, desires to enter the place where she is bathing; but it is forbidden to him to do this—so he is addressed by the *sakhī* who is trying to find a way to disguise him as a woman so he can enter the bath. However, it seems to be a nearly hopeless task.
2. Kṛṣṇa's lips are probably very red from betel juice.
3. Sun and moon are the symbols of "separation" and "union" in that order. In controlling them, Kṛṣṇa, upon entering the bath, would not show any particular emotion.
4. Kṛṣṇa always wears a necklace with the *kaustubhmaṇi,* a type of jewel, on his chest; concealing that in a silken cloth, the *sakhī* will rub his body with pollen to cover its dark color.
5. It will be very difficult for Kṛṣṇa to mask his joy at being reunited with Rādhā. She will become suspicious of his disguise because his joyful face will have the appearance of the moon coming out from behind the clouds.
6. Finally, even if all other tricks succeed, Rādhā will surely guess the truth when she notices the moon-like face of Kṛṣṇa burning hot when it should be cool.
7. Certain conventional eyebrow movements are associated with love play, probably from the *Nāṭya Śāstra.* The *khaṁjan* bird or wagtail is noted for its fickleness. For more on ornithological symbolism in Indian love poetry, see Charlotte Vaudeville, "Rāmāyaṇa Studies I. The Krauñca-vadha Episode in the Vālmīki Rāmāyaṇa," *Journal of the American Oriental Society* 83, no. 3 (September 15, 1963): 327.

STANZA FIFTEEN

1. *Sakhī* is speaking.
2. Rādhikā, diminutive of Rādhā.

STANZA SIXTEEN

1. Rādhā is being persuaded by the *sakhī* to go to meet with Kṛṣṇa.
2. *Rāsa Līlā.*
3. The Indian cuckoo, distinguished by its rollicking song.
4. *Koka Vidyā,* one of the technical studies of sex art.
5. *Abhinaya,* conventional gestures, and so on, of Indian classical dance.
6. The god of love, multiplied to the nth power, is no match for Rādhā and Kṛṣṇa.

STANZA SEVENTEEN

1. Enchanter, epithet of Kṛṣṇa.
2. Rādhā.

STANZA EIGHTEEN

1. Kṛṣṇa.
2. Kṛṣṇa is an incarnation of Viṣṇu to whom Brahmā and Umā's husband, i.e., Śiva, have bowed.
3. The Vedas or revealed scriptures of Hinduism.
4. *Na iti.* Possibly a reference to the qualityless Brahman with whom Viṣṇu in one of his aspects would be identified by theologians.

STANZA NINETEEN

1. Kṛṣṇa.
2. Kṛṣṇa.
3. Rādhā.
4. Mṛdaṁg, a type of drum.
5. A musical instrument.
6. Śyāmā. Feminine of Śyām, epithet of Kṛṣṇa; so here, Rādhā.

STANZA TWENTY

1. *Sakhī* is speaking.
2. Biṁba is a red fruit.

STANZA TWENTY-ONE

1. *Sakhī* is speaking.

STANZA TWENTY-TWO

1. Though eyes are often compared to *khaṁjan* birds, Rādhā's are worth the sacrifice of millions of them—hence are much more lively and attractive, as the rest of the stanza attests.

STANZA TWENTY-THREE

1. The attractive one, Kṛṣṇa.
2. Śiva wears the sickle-moon in his hair.

STANZA TWENTY-FOUR

1. Kṛṣṇa.

2. *Kalpataru* or *kalpavrkṣa* (probably the *pārijāta* or coral tree is meant), in Indra's heaven a tree yielding whatever might be desired. It was stolen by Kṛṣṇa and taken to Vṛndāvan (or Dvāraka). See *Viṣṇu Purāna,* trans. H. H. Wilson (Calcutta: Punthi Pustak, 1961), p. 460 ff.
3. Various fragrant flowers.
4. *Muni,* "a holy sage endowed with divine inspiration (either as a result of a divine nature within, or as the product of rigid abstraction and mortification)." J. D. Bate, *A Dictionary of the Hindee Language* (London: Trübner & Co., 1875), p. 589.

STANZA TWENTY-SIX

1. Kṛṣṇa. (*Sakhī* is speaking.)
2. Kāmadeva.
3. Jamunā.
4. Kṛṣṇa.
5. Kṛṣṇa.

STANZA TWENTY-SEVEN

1. A stringed, lutelike instrument.
2. A type of mouth-harp.
3. "The great Hindoo festival of the red powder (the grand jubilee and saturnalia of the Hindoos) held at the approach of the vernal equinox . . . " Bate, *Dictionary,* p. 804.
4. In order better to hear the song.
5. This stanza is the perfect summation of the joys in beholding Rādhā and Kṛṣṇa in the precious land of Vṛndāvan.

STANZA TWENTY-EIGHT

1. Spring.
2. Kṛṣṇa, literally, "Nanda's darling."

STANZA TWENTY-NINE

1. Her plait coiled around the back of her head appears like the mythical dragon Rāhu that during an eclipse may appear to devour the moon—in this case her moon-shaped coiffeur.
2. The poet says that while embracing Kṛṣṇa's neck, Rādhā's arms appear like the reflecting pool or edging that is created at the base of a beautiful tree. In other words, Rādhā's arms enhance Kṛṣṇa's appearance.
3. Rādhā is described here with that rather heavy, voluptuous beauty which is also favored in many styles of sculpture of the female figure in India.
4. The soles of the feet and palms of the hands of dancing girls are usually colored with a red dye.

STANZA THIRTY

1. *Viparit rati.* The woman is above.

STANZA THIRTY-THREE

1. The locks of their finger-shaped ringlets, hanging down, which can be compared to thieving bees, cannot conceal their eyes, which are red from lack of sleep due to lovemaking.

STANZA THIRTY-FOUR

1. Kṛṣṇa.

STANZA THIRTY-FIVE

1. Normally this would be the act of a woman whose body blessing is given by spreading the border of the *sāḍī* (sari). Because of its maternal function, a woman's body has a special holiness which can be symbolically imputed in a blessing. Hence, Harivaṁś is acting the part of a woman.

STANZA THIRTY-SIX

1. Kṛṣṇa.
2. A type of Indian musical composition.
3. The general feeling of bliss.
4. Kṛṣṇa.
5. *Tattāthei.* Probably the rendering of the rhythmic scheme of a dance noted for its passionate intensity.
6. Kṛṣṇa.

STANZA THIRTY-SEVEN

1. In this stanza Rādhā has to be persuaded to go to Kṛṣṇa. One might compare the mood here with that in the *Gītā Govinda* where it is generally Rādhā who sits in a bower pining for Kṛṣṇa's arrival.
2. *Viraha.*
3. Kṛṣṇa's suffering in separation from Rādhā causes him to find familiar objects full of menacing characteristics.
4. Kṛṣṇa is suddenly overwhelmed by the prospect of the "battle" ahead of him.

STANZA THIRTY-EIGHT

1. Again the structure of sexual relations is compared with a battle in which the lovers defeat the forces of Kāmadeva, the god of sexual desire, who is attacking them.

STANZA FORTY

1. Cool, sweet-smelling, and gentle.

STANZA FORTY-ONE

1. Here reference is made to Kṛṣṇa's role as suppliant for Rādhā's graces.
2. Kṛṣṇa. The idea is not completely clear. The main line of thought is that love, or *bhakti,* is available only to those who know it. As compared with true *bhakti,* which is Kṛṣṇa's love for Rādhā, the attraction of anything else for the devotee, that is, "numberless varieties of passionate women," is unsatisfactory. The closing lines are somewhat didactic and evidently are addressed to the reader: there is no permanent value in any worldly attachment but only in Kṛṣṇa.

STANZA FORTY-TWO

1. Another somewhat conventionally didactic poem. It can be construed to mean that it is through Kṛṣṇa that we can find the grace that leads to Rādhā.
2. Fourth Hindu month, July-August—the time of monsoon rains.

STANZA FORTY-THREE

1. Kṛṣṇa is speaking.
2. "The wood-apple tree *(Aegle marmelos)* and its fruit." Bate, *Dictionary,* p. 708.

STANZA FORTY-FOUR

1. The sixteen ornamentations given in the *Amarakośa,* Kāṇḍa 2 on "Manuṣyavarga," verses 1276-1294, are: (1) *cūḍāmaṇi,* (2) *vālapāśya,* (3) *lalāṭikā,* (4) *karnikā,* (5) *graivayakam,* (6) *lalannikā,* (7) muktāvalī, (8) *kaṭakam,* (9) *kaṅkaṇam,* (10) *keyuram,* (11) *kāñcī* or *mekhalā,* (12) *mañjiraḥ,* (13) *aṅgulīyakam,* (14) *nāsābharaṇam,* (15-16) *vastrālaṁkāram* (two). Ornaments are sometimes classified into four groups: (1) *āvedhyam,* for pierced nose or ears; (2) *bandhanīyam,*clasped around the head, hair, etc.; (3) *kṣepyam,*used for the arms and legs; (4) *ānopyam,* such things as necklaces which are slipped on.
2. Kṛṣṇa.

STANZA FORTY-FIVE

1. A clove-shaped jewel.
2. To enhance their whiteness.

STANZA FORTY-SEVEN

1. This is a hide-and-seek poem. Rādhā and Kṛṣṇa are together in the forest. Suddenly in her *līlā,* or sport, which includes the ability of divine beings to create illusions, Rādhā appears to be everywhere—in every leaf and flower petal.
2. Kṛṣṇa, the Greedy Bee, is anxious for sexual union with Rādhā; but he can no longer tell which is she and which is her mirror image.
3. Playing the illusion game of hide-and-seek makes Rādhā's desire for sexual union increase.
4. Finally, Rādhā gives herself away by putting a dark cosmetic line at her eyes which, in the mirror images, in some fashion, appears reversed—then Kṛṣṇa can tell which one is the real Rādhā.
5. Here the theme of the female companion is carried to its extreme. Kṛṣṇa at last considers himself to be one of the "friends." It is a mysterious idea.

STANZA FIFTY-ONE

1. Rādhā by withholding herself from Kṛṣṇa is robbing him of a measure of tribute which is his by virtue of his royal status. Then the poet goes on to list the priceless objects in question.

STANZA FIFTY-TWO

1. Not only in reverence but with a sense of defeat in the comparison of beauty.
2. Another example of how Rādhā takes precedence over Kṛṣṇa in the Rādhāvallabha ideology.

STANZA FIFTY-THREE

1. Rādhā is more powerful than Kṛṣṇa because of Kṛṣṇa's consuming passion for her.

STANZA FIFTY-FOUR

1. The repeated theme of newness and freshness, especially evident in this stanza but also frequently indicated elsewhere, creates the impression of an eternal time

of youth, of beginning, of agelessness. It also contributes to the special, static atmosphere of the stanzas. Working within a very limited range of metaphors and ideas, the poet nevertheless contrives marvelous variety, but somehow to the end that everything should remain the same in Rādhā and Kṛṣṇa's garden paradise.

STANZA FIFTY-FIVE

1. Rādhā's fair color against Kṛṣṇa's dark skin is frequently compared with lightning against the rain cloud. Here the comparison is even more explicit: Rādhā and the lightning itself compete for Kṛṣṇa's favor.
2. Defeated by Rādhā, the lightning gradually twinkles out.

STANZA FIFTY-SIX

1. Kāmadeva once annoyed Śiva (Paśupati), who burnt him up with a single ray from his powerful third eye.
2. Rādhā and Kṛṣṇa.

STANZA FIFTY-SEVEN

1. The forest of Vṛndāvan. *Śrī* is an honorific title.
2. Rādhā's paradise is Vṛndāvan and can only be obtained through her.
3. The most pleasant seasons, particularly in northern India where winter weather is often very cold and the summer heat completely unbearable. For a description of the latter, read Rudyard Kipling's short story, "City of Dreadful Night."
4. What follows here for several lines is a description in brief form of some of the activities of the spring festival or Holī.
5. A variant of Holī.
6. During Holī crowds of people in the streets throw colored powder and water on one another and also squirt each other with syringes filled with colors (see below). It is a time of abandonment of ordinary conduct when servants insult their masters, when Brahmins consume drinks prepared with *bhaṁg* or hemp, and when one may shout aloud obscenities and hilarious remarks. It can also be a time of violence, but the overall theme is of joy, fertility, and the rejuvenation of the earth.
7. Colored powder.

STANZA FIFTY-EIGHT

1. The tenth stage of *viraha* is death; so Kṛṣṇa is *in extremis* from longing for Rādhā. In these lines one of the female companions is again trying to persuade Rādhā to go to him.
2. The moon, the Lover of Rohinī.
3. Rādhā.
4. Kṛṣṇa (Hari), at the point of death from pangs of separation from Rādhā, will allow himself to receive his life, and so on, from her if she will bestow her love on him.

STANZA FIFTY-NINE

1. Another didactic stanza that seems to try to explain in nonmythic terms the reason for devotion to Rādhā and Kṛṣṇa.
2. An early courtesan who became famous for her piety. The point is that one who has many lovers cannot avoid difficulties.
3. Cf. *Kaṭha Upaniṣad.*

STANZA SIXTY

1. Kṛṣṇa's eyes. This stanza illustrates the theme that for Kṛṣṇa *viraha,* separation, the alternative state to *milana,* or union, is experienced in minute instances.
2. One *kalpa* is equivalent to 4,320,000,000 solar years; according to Hindu cosmology, it is the period of time equal to a single life of the universe. It is followed by an equal period of time of dissolution, after which the universe is created again.

STANZA SIXTY-ONE

1. Rādhā.
2. Kṛṣṇa.

STANZA SIXTY-TWO

1. Rādhā and Kṛṣṇa.
2. See note 5 of stanza thirty-six.

STANZA SIXTY-THREE

1. Tribhaṁgī, an epithet of Kṛṣṇa, referring to the three curves of his body in a dancing pose: (1) his head is tilted to one side; (2) his torso is tilted on one side; (3) one leg takes the body's weight and its knee bends to one side as the other leg is lifted somewhat off the ground on the other.
2. Here *darśan* means the "sight of." As a technical term it usually refers to glimpses of gods, holy persons, and great leaders.
3. "Bee-like play" is an allusion to lovemaking.
4. The stanza as a whole exemplifies very well the predominant role given to Kṛṣṇa in most sects that draw upon the accounts of his activities in the *Bhāgavata Purāṇa,* especially book X. Harivaṁś thereby does not mean to detract from his own commitment to the preeminence of Rādhā.

STANZA SIXTY-FOUR

1. Either the forest or the fig tree in or near which Kṛṣṇa leads the *rāsa līlā.*
2. "As a fish it might be conjectured to be the horned shark, or the unicorn fish; but it is often drawn, as in the pictured signs of the zodiac, with the head and forelegs of an antelope and the body and tail of a fish: it is the emblem of the god of love." Bate, *Dictionary,* p. 556.
3. A somewhat curious reference, in this context, to Kṛṣṇa as divine child.
4. Kṛṣṇa.

STANZA SIXTY-SIX

1. Kṛṣṇa is speaking to Rādhā. This stanza is ingenious in the way that it suggests the continual attraction of the divine lovers for each other and their unflagging desire in the midst of ceaseless lovemaking. Here, even though they have hardly stopped making love, except for a few brief moments when Rādhā sleeps in his lap, Kṛṣṇa has the impression that he must begin again to implore for her love; and he appears to have no recollection of their previous ecstasy.
2. Rādhā speaks in this line and the line above and tells Kṛṣṇa that the way to obtain her bliss is not by talking but by acting. In the lines following, Kṛṣṇa, who has no power of his own to acquire Rādhā's graces, falls into a state of confusion, feeling rejected and so on, and is restored only by Rādhā's condescending embrace.

STANZA SIXTY-SEVEN

1. These are often seen in Indian sculptured treatments of the female figure. They are three creases in the modelling of the skin on the abdomen and lend sensuous attraction.
2. The hearer.

STANZA SIXTY-EIGHT

1. The seven notes of the musical scale.

STANZA SIXTY-NINE

1. Rādhā and Kṛṣṇa.
2. Jamunā.
3. In other words, they keep silent in order to better hear the sound of Rādhā and Kṛṣṇa singing.

STANZA SEVENTY-ONE

1. See stanza sixty-four.
2. The moon slows down to witness Rādhā's dance.

STANZA SEVENTY-THREE

1. Red in the corner with a black pupil in the white.
2. Harivaṁś exhorts the goddess.

STANZA EIGHTY

1. Cowmaid.

STANZA EIGHTY-TWO

1. The conventional teachings of Hinduism.

The *Braj Bhāṣā* Text of the *Caurāsī Pad*

The text that follows is edited from Śrī Lalitācaraṇ Gosvāmī, *Śrī Hit Caurāsī* (Delhi: National Publishing House, 1963). The main change in this version is the harmonization of the orthography of substantives, particularly in the case of compounds, where, except in those instances in which a Sanskrit *sandhi* rule applies and necessitates the euphonic combination of vowels, the members of compounds are spaced or separated. This is done in an effort to correct the inconsistency in the previously published text in which compounds are sometimes spaced, sometimes unspaced, and sometimes joined with hyphens. There are also notes for certain words, many of which in the *Braj* text are the Hindi *tadbhava* forms of Sanskrit originals.

श्री हित चतुराशी[1]

जोई जोई प्यारौ करै सोई मोहि भावै,
भावै मोहि जोई सोई सोई करै प्यारे ॥
मोकों तौ भावती ठौर प्यारे के नैननि में,
प्यारौ भयो चाहै मेरे नैननि के तारे ॥
मेरे तन मन प्राण हूँ ते प्रीतम[2] प्रिय ,
अपने कोटिक प्राण प्रीतम मोसों हारे॥
जै श्री हित हरिवंश हंस हंसनि सांवल गौर[3],
कहौ कौन करै जल तरङ्गनि[4] न्यारे
॥ २ ॥

---

1 चौरासी
2. प्रियतम
3 गोर
4 जलतरङ्गणी

प्योर बोली भामिनी आजु नीकी जामिनी[1],
भैंटि नवीन मेघ सों दामिनी ॥
मोहन रसिक राइरी माई, तासों जु
मान करै ऐसी कौन कामिनी ॥
जै श्री हित हरिवंश श्रवण सुनत प्यारी,
राधिका रमण सों मिली गज गामिनी ॥
॥ २ ॥

प्रात समय[2] दोऊ रस लंपट[3]
सुरत जुद्ध[4] जय जुत[5] अति फूल ॥
श्रम वारिज घन बिन्दु वदन पर
भूषण अंग हि अंग विकूल[6]
कछु रह्यौ तिलक शिथिल अलकावलि[7]
वदन कमल मानौ अलि भूल ॥
जै श्री हित हरिवंश मदन रंग रंगि रहे
नैन बैन कटि शिथिल दुकूल ॥ ३ ॥

---

1 यामिनी
2 प्रातः काले
3. रस लंपट
4 सुरत युद्ध
5. युत or युक्त
6. विकल
7 कुन्तलनिचय

आजु तौ जुवति[1] तेरौ वदन आनन्द भरयौ,
पिय[2] के संगम के सूचत सुख चैन[3] ॥
आलस[4] वलित बोल[5] सुरंग रंगे कपोल[6]
विथकित[7] अरुण उनींदे दोऊ नैन[8] ॥
रुचिर तिलक लेश किरत कुसुम केश
शिर सीमंत भूषित मानों तैं न ॥
करुणाकर उदार राखत कछु न सार[9]
दसन वसन[10] लागत जब दैन ॥
काहे को दुरत भीरु पलटे प्रीतम चोर
बस किये श्याम सिखै सत मैन ॥
गलित उरसि माल[11] शिथिल किंकिनी जाल[12]
जै श्री हित हरिवंश लता गृह शैन[13]
॥ ४ ॥

---

1 युवति
2. प्रिय
3. सुखानन्द
4 सालस
5 वचन
6. रक्तकपोल
7. श्रान्ता
8 नयन
9 शेष
10 अधर
11 माला
12 किंकिणीसमूह
13. शयन

आजु प्रभात लता मन्दिर में,
सुख बरसत[1] अति हरखि[2] युगल वर।
गौर श्याम अभिराम रङ्ग भरे,
लटकि लटकि पग धरत अवनि[3] पर।
कुच कुमकुम रंजित मालावलि,
सुरत नाथ श्री श्याम धाम धर।
प्रिया प्रेम के अंक अलंकृत
चित्रित चतुर शिरोमणि[4] निजकर[5]॥
दम्पति[6] अति अनुराग मुदित[7]
कल गान करत मन हरत परस्पर।
जै श्री हित हरिवंश प्रसंस परायन[8],
गायन[9] अलि सुर देत मधुरतर॥५॥

---

1. वर्षत्
2. अतिप्रसन्न
3. भूमि
4. शिरसमणि
5. स्वहस्त
6. युगल
7. तुष्ट
8. प्रशंसातत्पर
9. भृङ्गगुञ्जन

कौन चतुर जुवती[1] प्रिया,
जाहि मिलत लाल चोर ह्वै रैन ।
दुरवत क्योंऽब दुरै सुनि प्यारे,
रंग में गहिले चैन में नैन ॥
उर[2] नख चन्द्र[3] बिराने[4],
पट अटपटे से बैन ।
जै श्री हित हरिवंश रसिक
राधापति प्रमथित मैन ॥६॥

आजु निकुंज[5] मंजु में खेलत,
नवल किशोर नवीन किशोरी ।
अति अनुपम अनुराग परस्पर,
सुनि अभूत भूतल पर जोरी ॥

---

1. युवति
2. उरस्
3. नखचन्द्र
4. अन्य
5. लतावितान

विद्रुम फटिक[1] विविध निर्मित घर,
नव कर्पूर पराग[2] न थोरी ।
कोमल किसलय शयन सुपेशल,
तापर श्याम निवेशित गोरी ॥
मिथुन हास परिहास परायन[3],
पीक कपोल कमल पर झोरी ।
गौर श्याम भुज कलह मनोहर,
नीवी बंधन मोचत डोरी ॥
हरि उर मुकुर[4] विलोकि अपनपौ
विभ्रम विकल मान जुत भोरी[5] ।
चिबुक सुचारु प्रलोइ प्रबोधत,
पिय[6] प्रतिबिंब जनाय निहोरी ॥
नेति नेति वचनामृत[7] सुनि सुनि,
ललितादिक[8] देखत दुरि चोरी ।
जै श्री हित हरिवंश करत कर धूनन[9],
प्रणयकोप मालावलि तोरी ॥ ७ ॥

1. स्फटिक
2. कर्पूरधूकी
3. परायण
4. दर्पण
5. राधा (भीरु)
6. प्रिय
7. वचन अमृत
8. ललिता अदिक
9. करताल

अति ही अरुण तेरे नैन नलिन[1] री ॥
आलस जुत इतरात रंग मगे,
भये निशि जागर मखिन मलिन री ॥
शिथिल पुलक में उठति गोलक गति
बिंधयौ मोहन मृग सकत चलि न री ॥
जै श्री हित हरिवंश हंस कल गामिनी,
संभ्रम देत भ्रमरनि अलिन[2] री ॥८॥

बनी श्री राधा मोहन की जोरी।
इन्द्रनीलमणि श्याम मनोहर सात कुम्भ[3] तनु
गोरी ॥
भाल विशाल तिलक हरि कामिनि चिकुर
चन्द्र बिच रोरी ॥
गज नायक प्रभु चाल गयंदनि गति वृषभानु
किशोरी

---

1. नयन कमलनी
२. आली
3. शात कुम्भ स्वर्ण

नील निचोल जुवति मोहन पट पीत अरुण
शिर खोरी ।
जै श्री हित हरिवंश रसिक राधापति
सुरत रंग में बोरी
॥ १९ ॥

आजु नागरी किशोर भावंती विचित्र जोर ,
कहा कहौं अंग अंग[1] परम माधुरी ॥
करत केलि कंठ मेलि बाहुदंड गंड गंड[2]
परस[3] सरस रास लास मण्डली जुरी ॥
श्याम सुन्दरी विहार बाँसुरी मृंदग तार ,
मधुर घोष नूपुरादि किंकिनी चुरी ॥
जै श्री देखत हरिवंश आलि निर्तनी सुधंग
चाल
वारि फेर देत प्राण देह सौं दुरी ॥२०॥

---

1. प्रत्यंङ्ग
2. प्रतिगंड
3. स्पर्श

मंजुल कल कुंज देश राधा हरि विशद वेश,
राका नभ कुमुद बंधु शरद जामिनी ।
सांवल दुति कनक अंग विहरत मिलि एक
संग,
नीरद मणि नील मध्य लसत दामिनी ॥
अरुण पीत नव दुकूल अनुपम अनुराग मूल,
सौरभयुत शीत अनिल मंद गामिनी ।
किसलय दल रचित शैन बोलत पिय[1]
चाटु बैन,
मान सहित प्रतिपद प्रतिकूल कामिनी ॥
मोहन मन मथत मार परसत[2] कुच नीवि
हार
वेपथयुत नेति नेति बदति[3] भामिनी
नर वाहन प्रभु सुकेलि बहुविधि भर भरत
झेलि
सौरत रस रूप नदी जगत पावनी
॥ ११ ॥

---

1. प्रिय 2. स्पृशति 3. वदति

चलहि राधिके सुजान तेरे हित सुख निधान,
रास रच्यौ श्याम तट कलिंद नंदिनी ।
निर्तत युवती समूह राग रंग अति कुतूह,[1]
बाजत रसमूल मुरलिका अनन्दिनी ॥
वंशीबट निकट जहां परम रमनि[2] भूमि
तहाँ,
सकल सुखद मलय बहै वायु मन्दिनी ।
जाती ईषद विकास कानन अतिशय सुवास,
राका निशि शरद मास विमल चंदिनी ।
नरवाहन प्रभु निहार लोचन भरि घोष
नारि[3],
नख शिख सौंदर्य काम दुख निकन्दिनी[4],
बिलसहु भुज ग्रीव मेलि भामिनि सुख
सिंधु झेलि,
नव निकुंज श्याम केलि जगत बन्दिनी[5] ॥
॥ २२ ॥

1. कौतूहल
2. रमणी
3. नारी
4. निकृन्तनी
5. वन्दिनी

नंद के लाल हरयौ मन मोर ।
हौं अपने मोतिन लर पोवति ,
कांकर डारि गयो सखि भोर ॥
बंक विलोकनि[1] चाल छबीली ,
रसिक शिरोमणि[2] नंद किशोर ।
कहि कैसे मन रहत श्रावन सुनि ,
सरस मधुर मुरली की घोर ।
इंदु गोविंद वदन के कारन[3]
चितवन कों भये नैन चकोर
जै श्री हित हरिवंश रसिक रस जुवती
तू लै मिलि सखी प्रान अकोर ॥ १३॥

---

1. विलोकते
2. शिरसमणि
3. कारण

अधर अरुण तेरे कैसे कै दुराऊं ।
रवि शशि शंक भजन कियौं अपवस ,
अद्भुत[1] रंगनि कुसुम बनाऊं
शुभ कौसेय[2] कसिब कौस्तुभमणि ,
पंकज सुतनु लै अंगनु लुपाऊं ।
हरषित[3] इंदु तजत जैसे जलधर ,
सो भ्रम ढूंढि कहां हौ पाऊं ।
अम्बुन[4] दम्भु कछू नहीं व्यापत[5] ,
हिमकर[6] तपै ताहि कैसे कै बुझाऊं
जै श्री हित हरिवंश रसिक नव रंग पिय[7] ,
भृकुटी भौंह तेरे खंजन लराऊं ॥१४॥

---

1. अद्भुत
2. कौशेय
3. हर्षित
4. अम्बु
5. व्याप्त
6. चन्द्र
7. प्रिय

अपनी बात मोसौं कहि री भामिनी ,
औंगी मौंगी रहति गरब[1] की माती[2] ।
हौं तोसौं कहत हारी सुनि री राधिका प्यारी,
निशि को रंग क्यों न कहत लजाती ।
गलित कुसुम बैनी सुनि री सारंग नैनी ,
छूटी लट अचरा बदति[3] अलसाती ।
अधर निरंग रंग रच्यौ री कपोलनि ,
जुवति चलति गजगति अरुझाती ,
रहसि रमी छबीले रसन बसन ढीले ,
शिथिल कसनि कंचुकी उर राती ।
सखी सौं सुनि श्रवन बचन ,
मुदित मन चली हरिवंश भवन
मुसिकाती ॥२५॥

---

1. गर्व
2. मत्त
3. वदति

आजु मेरे कहे चलौ मृगनैनी ।
गावत सरस जुवति मंडल में,
पिअ[1] सौं मिलै भलै पिक बैंनी ।
परम प्रवीन[2] कोक विद्या में
अभिनय निपुन[3] लाग गति लैनी,
रूपरासि[4] सुनि नवल किशोरी,
पल पल घटति चाँदनी रैनी ।
जै श्री हित हरिवंश चली अति
आतुर
राधा रमण सुरत सुख दैनी ।
रहसि रभस आलिंगन चुम्बन,
मदन कोटि कुल भई कुचैनी
॥ १६ ॥

---

1. प्रिय
2. प्रवीण
3. निपुण
4. राशि

आजु देखि ब्रज सुन्दरी मोहन बनी
केलि ।
अंस अंस[1] बाहु दै किशोर जोर रूप
रासि[2] ।
मनौ तमाल अरुझि रही सरस कनक
बेलि ।
नव निकुंज भ्रमर कुंज मंजु घोष
प्रेम पुंज,
गान करत मोर पिकनि अपने सुर
सों मेलि ।
मदन मुदित अंग अंग बीच बीच
सुरत रंग,
पल पल हरिवंश पिवत नैन चषक
झेलि ॥

॥ १७ ॥

---

1. अंस :
2. राशि

सुनि मेरो वचन छबीली राधा ।
तैं पायौ रस सिंधु अगाधा[1],
तू वृषभानु गोप की बेटी
जाहि बिरंचि[2] उमा पति नाये,
तापै तैं बन फूल बिनाये ।
जो रस नेति नेति श्रुति भाख्यौ[3],
ता कौ तैं अधर सुधारस चाख्यौ ।
तेरौ रूप कहत नहीं आवै ।
जै श्री हित हरिवंश कछुक जस[4] गावै ॥

॥ १८ ॥

खेलत रास रसिक व्रज मंडन,
जुवतिन अंस दिये भुज दंडन ।
शरद विमल नभ चन्द्र विराजै,
मधुर मधुर मुरली कल बाजै ।
अतिराजत घन श्याम तमाला
कंचन[5] बेलि बनी व्रज बाला ।

---

1 अगाध   3. श्रुतिगदित
2. विरिञ्चि   4. यश   5. काञ्चन

बाजत ताल मृदंग उपंगा
गान मथत मन कोटि अनंगा ।
भूषन बहुत विविध रंग सारी
अँग सुधंग दिखावत नारी
बरषत[1] कुसुम मुदित सुरयोषा
सुनियत दिवि दुन्दुभि कल घोषा ।
जै श्री हित हरिवंश मगन[2] मन श्यामा,
राधा रवण सकल सुख धामा ॥

॥ २९ ॥

मोहनलाल के रसमाती ।
बधू[3] गुपति गोपति कत मोसौं प्रथम नेह
सकुचाती ॥
देखि संभार पीत पट ऊपर कहाँ चूनरी
राती ।
टूटी लर लटकत मोतिन की नख[4] विधु
अंकित छाती ॥

---

1. वर्षति
2. मग्न
3. वधू
4. नखेन्दु

अधर बिंब खंडित, मषि मंडित गंड, चलति
अरुझाती ।
अरुण नैंन घूमत आलय जुत, कुसुम गलित
लटपाती ॥
आजु रहसि मोहन सब लूटी, विविध
आपुनी थाती ।
जै श्री हित हरिवंश वचन सुनि भामिनि,
भवन चली मुसिकाती ॥
॥ २० ॥

तेरे नैंन करत दोउ चारी ।
अति कुलकात समात नहीं,
कहुँ मिले हैं कुंजबिहारी[1] ॥
बिथुरी माँग, कुसुम गिरि गिरि परैं,
लटकि रही लट न्यारी ।
उर नख रेख प्रगट[2] देखियत है,
कहा दुरावत प्यारी ॥
परी है पीक सुभग गंडनि पर,

---

1 विहारी 2. प्रकट

अधर निरंग सुकुमारी ।
जै श्री हित हरिवंश रसिकनी
भामिनि ,
आलस अंग अंग भारी ॥ २१ ॥

नैननि पर वारौं कोटिक खंजन ।
चंचल चपल अरुण अनियारे अग्रभागवन्यौ
अंजन ॥
रुचिर मनोहर वक्र विलोकन सुरत
समर दल गंजन ।
जै श्री हित हरिवंश कहत न बनै छवि
सुख समुद्र मनरंजन ॥
॥ २२ ॥
राधा प्यारी तेरे नैन सलोल[1]
तैं निज भजन कनक तन जोवन[2] लियो
मनोहर मोल
अधर निरंग अलक लट छूटी रंजित पीक
कपोल ॥

1. लोल , चञ्चल 2. यौवन

तू रस मगन भई नहिं जानत, ऊपर पीत
निचोल ॥
कुच युग पर नख रेख प्रगट मानों शंकर
शिर शशि टोल ।
जै श्री हित हरिवंश कहत कछु भामिनि
अति आलस सों बोल ॥
॥ २३ ॥

आजु गोपाल रास रस खेलत,
पुलिन कल्पतरु तीर री सजनी ।
शरद विमल नभ चन्द्र विराजत,
रोचक त्रिविध समीर री सजनी
चंपक बकुल मालती मुकुलित,
मत्त मुदित पिक कीर री सजनी ॥
देशी सुधँग राग रँग नीकौ,
व्रज जुवतिन की भीर री सजनी ॥
मघवा मुदित निसान बजायो,
व्रत छांड्यो मुनि धीर री सजनी ।

जै श्री हित हरिवंश मगन¹ मन श्यामा ,
हरत मदन धन पीर री सजनी ॥

॥ २४ ॥

आजु नीकी बनी राधिका नागरी ।
ब्रज जुवति जूथ² में रूप अरु चतुरई ,
सील³ सिंगार⁴ गुन⁵ सवन तें आगरी ॥
कमल दक्षिण भुजा वाम भुज अंस सखि ,
गावति⁶ सरस मिलि मधुर स्वर राग री ।
सकल विद्या विदित रहसि हरिवंश हित ,
मिलत नव कुंज वर श्याम बड भागरी ॥

॥ २५ ॥

मोहनी मदन गोपाल की बांसुरी ।
माधुरी श्रवण पुट सुनत सुनि राधिके ।
करत रति राज के तापकौ नासुरी ॥
सरद⁷ राका रजनि विपिन वृन्दा सजनि ,

---

1. मग्न
2. यूथ
3. शील
4. शृंगार
5. गुण
6. गायति
7. शरद्

अनिल अतिमंद सीतल[1] सहित बासुरी ।

परम पावन पुलिन भृंगसेवित नलिन,

कल्पतरु तीर बलवीर कृत रासु री ॥

सकल मण्डल भलीं तुम जु हरिसों मिलीं

बनी वर वनित उपमा कहौं कासु री

तुम जु कंचनतनी[2] लाल मर्कतमनी[3]

उभै[4] कलहंस हरिवंश बलि दासु री ॥

॥ २६ ॥

मधु ऋतु वृन्दावन आनंद नथोर ।

राजत नगरी नव कुशल किशोर ॥

यूथिका युगक[5] रूप मञ्जरी रसाल

विकथित आलि मधु माधवी गुलाल ।

चंपक बकुल कुल विविध सरोज

केतकी मेदिनी मद मुदित मनोज ॥

रोचक रुचिर बहै त्रिविध समीर

मुकुलित नूत नदत पिक कीर ॥

---

1. शीतल 3. मरकतमणि 5. द्विरूप

2. काञ्चनतनु 4. उभ

पावन पुलिन घन मंजुल निकुंज
किसलय शैन रचित सुख पुंज ॥
मंजीर मुरज डफ मुरली मृदंग
बाजत उपंग बीणा वर मुख चंग ॥
मृगमद मलयज कुंकुम अबीर
बंदन अगरसत सुरंगित चीर ॥
गावत सुन्दरि हरि सरस धमारि
पुलकित खग मृग बहत न बारि
जै श्री हित हरिवंश हंस हंसिनी समान
ऐसे ही करौ मिलि जुग जुग[1] राज ॥

॥ २८ ॥

राधे देखि बनकी बात

ऋतु बसंत अनंत मुकुलित कुसुम अरु फल पात ॥
बेणु धुनि[2] नंदलाल बोली सुनि ब क्यों अरसात ।
करत कतब विलम्ब भामिनि बृथा औसर[3] जात ॥

---

1 युग युग 2. ध्वनि 3. अवसर

लाल मर्कतमणि छबीलौ तुम जु कंचन गात[1]।
बनी श्रीहित हरिवंश जोरी उभय गुण गण मात॥
॥२८॥

ब्रज नव तरुणि कदम्ब मुकुटमणि श्यामा आजु बनी ॥
नखशिखलौं अँग अँग माधुरी मोहे श्याम घनी ॥
यौं राजत कबरी गूंथित कच, कनक कंज[2] वदनी ॥
चिकुर चंद्रिकनि बीच अर्ध बिधु[3] मानो ग्रासित फनी[4]
सौभग रस शिर श्रावत पनारी, पिय सीमन्त ठनी ॥
भृकुटि काम कोदण्ड, नैन सर, कज्जल रेख अनी ॥
तरल तिलक, ताटंक गंड पर, नासा जलज मनी[5] ॥

---

1. गात्र
2. कमल
3. अर्धेन्दु
4. फणी
5. मौक्तिक

दसन कुंद सरसाधर[1] पल्लव प्रीतम मन
शामनी ॥
चिबुक मध्य अति चारू सहज सखि सांवल
बिंदुकनी ॥
प्रीतम प्राण रतन संपुट कुच कञ्चुकि कसिब
तनी ॥
भुज मृनाल[2] बल हरत वलय जुत[3] परस[4]
सरस श्रवनी ॥
श्याम शीश तरू मनौं मिडवारी रची रूचिर
रवनी ॥
नाभि गंभीर मीन मोहन मन खेलत कौं
हृदनी ॥
कृश कटि पृथु नितम्ब किंकिणि व्रत कदलि
खंभ[5] जघनी ॥
पद अम्बुज जावक जुत भूषन प्रीतम उर
अवनी ॥

---

1. सरस अधर
2. मृणाल
3. युत
4. स्पर्श
5. स्तम्भ

नव नव भाय विलोभि भाम इभ विहरत
बर करनी ॥
जै श्री हित हरिवंश प्रशंसत श्यामा कीरत
विशद घनी ॥
गावत श्रवन सुनत सुखाकर विश्व दुरित
दवनी[1] ॥२९॥

देखत नव निकुंज सुनि सजनी लागत है
अति चारु ।
माधविका केतुकी लता लै रच्यौ मदन
आगारु[2] ॥
सरद मास राका निशि शीतल मन्द सुगन्ध
समीर ,
परिमल लुब्ध मधुव्रत विथकित नदत
कोकिला कीर ॥
बहुविधि रंग मृदुल किसलय दल निर्मित
पिय सखि सेज ।

1 दमनी 2. अगार गृह

भाजन कनक विविध मधुपूरित धरे धरनि
पर हेज ॥
तापर कुशल किशोर किशोरी करत हास
परिहास ।
प्रीतम पाणि उरज वर परसत प्रिया दुरावत
वास ।
कामिनि कुटिल भृकुटि अवलोकत दिन
प्रतिपद प्रतिकूल ।
आतुर अति अनुराग विवस[1] हरि धाई धरत
भुज मूल ॥
जागर नीवी बंधन मोचन ऐंचत नील
निचोल ॥
वधू कपट हठ कोप कहत कल नेति
नेति मधु बोल ॥
परिरंभन विपरित रति वितरत सरस सुरत
निजु केलि ।
इन्द्रनीलमणिमय तरु मानों लसत कनक
की बेलि ॥

---

1 विवश।

रतिरण मिथुन ललाट पटल पर श्रमजल-
सीकर[1] संग
ललितादिक[2] अंचल झकझोरत मन
अनुराग अभंग ॥
जै श्री हित हरिवंश यथामति वरनत[3]
कृष्ण रसामृत[4] सार ।
श्रवन सुनत प्रापक रति राधा पद
अम्बुज सुकुमार ॥३०॥

आजु अति राजत दंपति[5] भोर ।
सुरत रंग के रस में भीने नागरि नवल
किशोर ॥
अंसनि पर भुज दीये विलोकत इंदु
वदन विवि[6] ओर ।
करत पान रस मत्त परस्पर लोचन
तृषित चकोर ॥

---

1 शीकर 3. वर्णित 5. दम्पती

2. ललिताआदिक 4. रस अमृत 6. विधि

छूटी लटनि लाल मन करष्यौ ये याके
चित चोर ।
परिरम्भन चुम्बन मिलि गावत सुर
मंदर कल घोर ॥
पग डगमगत चलत बन विहरत रुचिर
कुंज घन खोर
जै श्री हित हरिवंश लाल ललना मिलि
हियौ सिरावत मोर ॥

॥ ३२ ॥

आजु बन क्रीडत श्यामा श्याम
सुभग बनी निशि शरद चांदनी रुचिर
कुंज अभिराम ॥
खंडन अधर करत परिरम्भन ऐंचत
जघन दुकूल ।
उर नख पात तिरिछी चितवनि दंपति
रस समतुल ॥
वे भुज पीन पयोधर परसत वामदृशा
पिय[1] हार ।

1 प्रिय

बसननि पीक[1] अलक आकर्षत समर
श्रमित सत मार ।
पल पल प्रबल चौप रस लम्पट अतिसुन्दर
सुकुमार ॥
जै श्री हित हरिवंश आजु तृण टूटत
हौ बलि विशद विहार ॥
॥ ३२ ॥

आजु बन राजत जुगल[2] किशोर ।
नन्द नन्दन वृषभानु नन्दिनी उठे उनीदे
भोर ॥
डगमगात पग परत शिथिल गति परसत
नख शशि छोर ।
दसन बसन खण्डित मषि मण्डित गण्ड
तिलक कछु थोर ॥
दुरत न कच करजन[3] के रोके अरुन
नैन अलि चोर ।
जै श्री हित हरिवंश संभार न तन मन
सुरत समुद्र झकोर ॥ ३३॥

1. पिक 2. युगल 3. अङ्की

बन की कुंजनि कुंजनि डोलनि
निकसत निपट सांकरी बीथिनि परसत
नाहि निचोलनि ।
प्रात काल रजनी सब जागे सूचत सुख
दृग[1] लोलनि ।
आलसवन्त अरुण अति व्याकुल कछु
उपजत गति गोलनि ।
निर्तन भृकुटि बदन अम्बुज मृदु सरस
हास मधु बोलनि ।
अति आसक्त लाल अलि लंपट बस
कीने बिनु मोलनि ॥
विलुलित[2] शिथिल श्याम छूटी लट राजत
रुचिर कपोलनि ॥
रति विपरित[3] चुम्बन परिरम्भन चिबुक
चारु टक टोलनि ॥

---

1. दृक्
2. विलुलित
3. विपरीत

कबहुं श्रमित किसलय सिज्या पर मुख
अंचल झक झोलनि ।
दिन हरिवंश दासि हिय सींचत वारिधि[1]
केलि कल्लोलनि[2] ॥३४॥

झूलत दोऊ नवल किशोर ।
रजनी जनित रंग सुख सूचत अंग अंग
उठि भोर ॥
अति अनुराग भरे मिलि गावत सुर मंदर
कल घोर ॥
वीच वीच प्रीतम चित चोरत प्रिया नैन
की कोर ॥
अबला अति सुकुमारि डरत मन वर
हिंडोर झकोर ।
पुलकि पुलकि प्रीतम उर लागत दै
नव उरज अंकोर ॥

---

1 समुद्र 2. कल्लोल

अरुझी विमल माल कंकन सों कुण्डल सों
कच डोर ।
बेपथ जुत क्यों बनै विवेचित आनंद बढ्यो
न थोर ॥
निरखि निरखि फूलत ललितादिक[1]
विधिमुख चन्द्र चकोर।
दै असीस हरिवंश प्रशंसत करि अंचल
की छोर ॥ ३५ ॥

आज बन नीको रास बनायौ ।
पुलिन पवित्र सुभग यमुना तट मोहन
बेनु[2] बजायौ ॥
कल कंकन किंकिनि नूपुर धुनि सुनि
खग मृग सचु पायौ ।
जुवतिनु मण्डल मध्य श्याम घन सारंग
राग जमायौ ॥
ताल मृदंग उपंग मुरज डफ मिलि रस
सिन्धु बढायौ ।

1 ललिताआदिक 2 वेणु

विविधि विशद वृषभानु नन्दिनी अङ्ग

सुधङ्ग दिखायौ ॥

अभिनय निपुन लटकि लट लोचन भृकुटि

अनंग नचायौ ।

तत्ताथेई धरति नूतन गति पति ब्रजराज

रिझायौ ॥

सकल उदार नृपति चूडामणि सुख वारिद[1]

बरसायौ ।

परिरम्भन चुम्बन आलिंगन उचित जुवति[2]

जन पायौ ॥

बरसत कुसुम मुदित नभनायक इंद्र

निसान बजायौ ।

जै श्री हित हरिवंश रसिक राधापति

जस वितान[3] जग छायौ ॥

॥ ३६ ॥

---

1. मेघ
2. युवति
3. यशोवितान

चल हि किन मानिनि कुंज कुटीर।
तौ बिनु कुंवर कोटि वनिता जुत मथत मदन की पीर॥
गदगद सुर[2] विरहाकुल[3] पुलकित श्रवत विलोचन नीर।
क्वासि[4] क्वासि वृषभानु नान्दिनी विलपत विपिन अधीर॥
वंशी विसिख[5] व्याल माला बलि पंचानन पिक कीर।
मलयज गरल हुतासन[6] मारुत साखामृग[7] रिपु चीर॥
जै श्री हित हरिवंश परम कोमल चित[8] चपल चली पिय तीर।
सुनि भयभीत ब्रजको पंजर सुरत सूर[9] रणवीर॥३७॥

---

1. युक्त
2. स्वर
3. विरह आकुल
4. क्व असि क्व असि
5. विशिख, बाण
6. हुताशन
7. शाखामृग
8. चित्त
9. शूर

बेहि चलहि उठि गहर करत कत निकुंज
बुलावत लाल ।
हा राधा राधिका पुकारत निरखि मदन
गज ढाल ।
करत सहाय सरद[1] ससि[2] मारुत फूटि मिली
उर माल ॥
दुर्गम तकत समर अति कातर करहि न
पिय[3] प्रति पाल ॥
जै श्री हित हरिवंश चली अति आतुर
श्रवन सुनत ते हि काल ॥
लै राखे गिरि कुच बिच सुन्दर सुरत
सूर ब्रज बाल ॥ ३८ ॥

खेल्यौ लाल चाहत रवन ।
रचि रचि अपने हाथ[4] संवार्यौ निकुञ्ज
भवन ॥

---

1. शरत्
2. शशी
3. प्रिय
4. हस्त

रजनी सरद मंद सौरभ सों सीतल[1] पवन ।
तो विनु कुंवरि कामकी वेदन मेटव कचन ॥
चलहि न चपल वाल मृग नैनी तजिव मवन[2] ।
जै श्री हित हरिवंश मिलव प्यारे की आरति
दवन ॥ ३९॥

बैठे लाल निकुञ्ज भवन ।
रजनी रुचिर मल्लिका मुकुलित त्रिविध पवन॥
तू सखि काम केलि मन मोहन मदन दवन ।
वृथा गहर कत करति कृशोदरि कारन[3] कवन ॥
चपल चली तन[4] की सुधि बिसरी सुनत श्रवन।
जै श्री हित हरिवंश मिले रस लंपट रधिका[5]
रवन ॥ ४०॥

---

1. शीतल
2. मौन
3. कारण
4 तनु
5. राधिका

प्रीति की रीति रंगी लौई जानै ।
जद्यपि[1] सकल लोक चूडामणि दीन अपनपौ
मानै ॥
जमुना पुलिन निकुंज भवन में मान मानिनी
ठानै ।
निकट नवीन कोटि कामिनि कुल धीरज मन
हि न आनै ॥
नस्वर[2] नेह चपल मधुकर ज्यों आन सों
बानै ।
जै श्री हित हरिवंश चतुर सोई लाल हिं
छांडि मैंड पहिचानै ॥
॥ ४२ ॥

प्रीति न काहु की कानि विचारै
मारग अपमारग[3] विथकित मन को अनुसरत
निवारै ॥
ज्यों सरिता सावन जल उमगत सनमुख
सिन्धु सिधारै ॥

---

1 यद्यपि 2 नश्वर 3. मार्ग, अपमार्ग

ज्यों नादहि मन दिये कुरंगनि प्रगट[1]
पारधी मारै ॥
जै श्री हित हरिवंश हिलग सारंग ज्यों
सलभ[2] सरीरहि जारै ।
नायिक[3] निपुन नवल मोहन विनु कौन
अपनपौ हारै ॥ ४१ ॥

अति नागरि वृषभानु किशोरी ।
सुनु दूतिका चपल मृग नैनी ॥
आकर्षत चितवत चित गोरी ।
श्री फल उरज कंचन सौ देहो ,
कटि केहरि गुणसिन्धु झकोरी ।
बैनी भुजंग चन्द्र सत वदनी ,
कदली जंघ जलचर गति चोरी ॥
सुनि हरिवंश आज रजनी मुख ,
वन मिलाइ मेरी निज जोरी ।

---

1 प्रकट 2. शलभ 3. नायक

यद्यपि मान समेत भामिनी ,
सुनि कत रहत भली जिय भोरी ॥४३॥

चलि सुन्दरि बोली वृन्दावन
कामिनि कण्ठ लागि किनि राजहि ,
तू दामिनि मोहन नूतन घन ॥
कंचुकि सुरंग विविध रंग सारी ,
नख जुग[1] ऊन बने तेरे तन ।
ये सब उचित नवल मोहन कौं ,
श्री फल कुच जोबन[2] आगम घन ॥
अतिसय[3] प्रीति हुती अन्तर गति ,
जै श्री हित हरिवंश चली मुकुलित[4] मन
निबिड निकुन्ज मिलै रस सागर[5]
जीते सत रतिराज सुरत रन ॥४४॥

---

1 युग
2 यौवन
3. अतिशय
4. मुकुक्कित
5. समुद्र

आवति श्री वृषभानु दुलारी ।

रूप रासि अति चतुर सिरोमनि[1] अंग अंग

सुकुमारी ॥

प्रथम उबटि मज्जन करि सज्जित नील बरन[2]

तन सारी ।

गूंथित अलक तिलक कृत सुन्दर सैंदुर

मांग संवारी ॥

मृगज समान नैन[3] अंजन जुत[4] रुचिर रेख

अनुसारी ।

जटित लवंग ललित नासा[5] पर दसनावलि[6]

कृतकारी ॥

श्री फल उरज कसुंभी[7] कंचुकि कसि ऊपर

हार छवि न्यारी

---

1. शिरस मनि
2. वर्ण
3. नयन
4. युत
5. नासिका
6. दशनावलि
7. कौसुम्भ

कृश कटि उदर गंभीर नाभिपुट जघन
नितम्बनि भारी
मनौ मृनाल[1] भूषन भूषित भुज श्याम अंस
पर डारी
जै श्री हित हरिवंश जुगल करनी गज
विहरत बन पिय[2] प्यारी ॥ ४५॥

विपिन घन कुंज रति केलि भुज मेलि रुचि,
श्याम श्यामा मिले सरद की जामिनी ।
हृदै[3] अति फूल सम तूल पिय नागरी,
करिनि करि मत्त मनों विविध गुन रामिनी॥
सरस गति हास परिहास आवेश बस
दलित दल मदन बल कोक रस कामिनी ।
जै श्री हित हरिवंश सुनि लाल लावन्य[4]
भिदे
प्रिया अति सूर सुख सुरत संग्रामिनी ॥
॥ ४६॥

1 मृणाल
2. प्रिय
3. हृदय
4. लावण्य

बनकी लीला लालहि भावै ।
पत्र प्रसून बीच प्रतिबिंबहिं नख सिख
प्रिया जनावै ।
सकुचन सकत प्रगट परिरंभन अलि
लम्पट दुरि धावै ॥
संभ्रम देत कुलकि कल कामिनि रति रण
कलह मचावै ॥
उलटि सबै समुझि नैननि में अंजन रेख
बनावै ।
जै श्री हित हरिवंश पिरीत[1] बस सजनी
श्याम कहावै ॥४७॥

बनी वृषभानु नन्दिनी आजु ।
भूषन बसन विविध पहिरे तन पिय मोहन हित
साजु ॥
हाव भाव[2] लावन्य भृकुटि लट हरत जुवति[3]
जन पाजु ।

1 प्रीति 2. भाव हाव 3. युवति

ताल भेद अवघर सुर[1] सूचत नूपुर किंकिनि
बाजु ॥
नव निकुन्ज अभिराम श्याम संग नीकौ
बन्यौ समाजु
जै श्री हित हरिवंश विलास रास जुत
जोरो अविचल राजु ॥
॥ ४८ ॥

देखि सखी राधा पिय[2] केलि ।
ये दोउ[3] खोरि खिरक गिरि गहवर[4]
विहरत कुंवर कंठ भुज मेलि ॥
ये दोउ नवल किशोर रूप निधि,
बिटप तमाल कनक मनों बेलि,
अधर अदन[5] चुम्बन परिरम्भन
तन पुलकित आनंद रस झेलि ॥
पट बंधन कन्चुकि कुच परसत
कोप कपट निरखत कर पेलि

1. स्वर
2. राधाप्रिया
3. द्वौ
4. गहवर
5. खण्डन

जै श्री हित हरिवंश लाल रस लम्पट ,
धाइ धरत उर बीच सकेलि ॥ ४९॥

नवल नागरि नवल नागर किशोर मिलि
कुञ्ज कोमल कमल दलनि सिज्या रची ।
गौर सांवल अंग रुचिर तापर मिले ,
सरस मणि नील मनों मृदुल कंचन खची ॥
सुरत नीवी निबन्ध हेत प्रिय मानिनी ,
प्रिया की भुजनि में कलह मोहन मची ।
सुभग श्री फल उरज पानि परसत रोष ,
हुंकार गर्व दृग भंगि भामिनि लची ॥
कोक कोटिक रभस रहसि हरिवंश हित ,
विविध कल माधुरी किमपि नाहिन बची ॥
प्रणयमय[1] रसिक ललितादि[2] लोचन चषक ,
पिवत मकरंद सुख रासि अंतर सची ॥ ५०॥

---

1 प्रणयसहित

२. ललिता आदि

दान दै री नवल किशोरी ।
माँगत लाल लाड़िलौ नागर ,
प्रगट भई दिन दिन की चोरी ॥
नव नारंग कनक हीरावलि ,
विद्रुम सरस जलज मनि[1] गोरी ।
पूरित रस पीयूष जुगल घट ,
कमल कदलि खंजन की जोरी ॥
तो पै सकल सौंज दामनि की ,
कत सतराति कुटिल दृग मोरी ।
नूपुर रव किंकिनी पिसुन घर ,
जै श्री हित हरिवंश कहत नहिं थोरी ॥
॥ ५२ ॥

देखो माई[2], सुन्दरता की सीवाँ ।
व्रज नवतरुनि कदंब नागरी ,
निरखि करत अधग्रीवाँ ॥
जो कोऊ कोटि कलप लगि जीवै ,
रसना कोटिक पावै ।

1. मौक्तिक 2. माता

तऊ रुचिर वदनारविंद[1] की
सोभा[2] करत न आवै ॥
देवलोक भूलोक रसातल
सुनि कवि कुल मति डरिये ।
सहज माधुरी अंग अंग की
कहि का सौं पटतरिये ॥
जै श्री हित हरिवंश प्रताप रूपगुण
वय बल श्याम उजागर ।
जाकी भ्रूविलास बस पशुरिव
दिन विथकित रस सागर ॥ ५२ ॥

देखो माई अवला कै बल रासि[3] ।
अति गज मत्त निरंकुस[4] मोहन निरखि
बंधे लट पासि ।
अब ही पंगु भई मनकी गति बिनु उद्दिम[5]
अनियास[6]

1. वदन अरविंद
2. शोभा
3. राशि
4. निरंकुश
5. उद्यम
6. अनायास

तव की कहा कहौ जब पिय प्रति चाहत
भृकुटि विलास ॥
कचसंजमन[1] ब्याज[2] भुज दरसति[3] मुसिकन
वदन विकास
हा हरिवंश अनीत रीति हित कत डारत
तन त्रास ॥५३॥

नयौ नेह नव रंग नयौ रस नवल श्याम
वृषभानु किशोरी ।
नव पीताम्बर नवल चूनरी नई नई बूंदन
भीजत गोरी ॥
नव वृन्दावन हरित मनोहर नव चातक
बोलत मोर मोरी ।
नव मुरली जु मलार नई गति श्रवन
सनत आये घनघोरी

1 संयमन 3 दर्शयति
2. व्याज

नव भूषण नव मुकुट विराजत नई नई
उरप लेत थोरी थोरी
जै श्री हित हरिवंश अशीष देत मुख चिर
जीवौ भूतल यह जोरी ॥
॥ ५४ ॥

आज दोऊ दामिनि मिलि बहसी ।
बिच लैं श्याम घटा अति नूतन ताकि
रंग रसी ॥
एक चमकि चहुं ओर सखीरी अपने सुभाय
लसी ।
आई एक सरस गहनी में दुहुं[1] भुज बीच बसी ॥
अम्बुज नील उभय विधु राजत तिनकी चलन
खसी ।
जै श्री हित हरिवंश लोभ भेटन मन पूरन
सरद ससी ॥ ५५ ॥

---

1 द्वौ

हौं बलि जाऊं नागरी श्याम ।
ऐसे ही रंग करौ निशि वासर वृन्दा विपिन
कुटी अभिराम ।
हास विलास सुरत रस सींचन पशुपति दग्ध
जिवातव काम ॥
जै श्री हित हरिवंश लोल लोचन अलि करहु
न सफल सकल सुख धाम ॥

॥ ५६ ॥

प्रथम यथामति प्रणऊं श्री वृन्दावन अतिरम्य ।
श्री राधिका कृपा बिनु सबके मननि अगम्य[1] ॥
वर यमुना जल सींचन दिन ही सरद बसंत
विविध भांति सुमनस के सौरभ अलिकुल मंत[2]
अरुण नूत पल्लव पर कूजत कोकिल कीर
निर्तन करत सिखीकुल[3] अति आनन्द अधीर॥
वहत पवन रुचि दायक सीतल मंद सुगंधु[4]
अरुण नील सित मुकुलित जहां तहां पूषन बंधु[5]॥

---

1 दुरूह
2. मत्त
3 शिखीकुल
4. सुगन्ध
5. कमल

अति कमनीय विराजत मंदिर नवल निकुञ्ज।
सेवत सगान[1] प्रीतिजुत दिन मीनध्वज पुञ्ज॥
रसिक रासि जहां खेलत श्यामा श्याम किशोर
उभै बाहु परिरंजित उठे उनींदे भोर ॥
कनक कपिस[2] पर सोभित सुभग सांवरे अंग।
नील बसन[3] कामिनि उर कंचुकी कसूंभी सुरंग।
ताल रबाब मुरज डफ बाजत मधुर मृदंग ॥
सरस उकति गति सूचत वर बंसुरी मुख
चंग।
दोउ मिलि चांचर गावत गौरी राग अलापि।
मानस मृग बल बेधत भृकुटि धनुष दृग
चांपि ॥
दोऊ कर तारिनु पटकत लटकत इत उत
जात ।
हो हो होरी बोलत अति आनंद कुल कात ॥
रसिक लाल पर मेलत कामिनि बंदन धूरी।

---

1. सगुण 2. कपिश। 3. वसन

पिय[1] पिचकारिनु छिरकत तकि तकि कुम कुम
पूरी ।
कबहुं कबहुं चन्दनतरु निर्मित तरल हिन्दोल
चढ़ि दोऊ जन झूलत फूलत करत कलोल ॥
बर हिंडोल झकोरनि कामिनि अधिक डरात
पुलकि पुलकि वेपथ अंग प्रीतम उर लपटात ॥
हितचिंतक निजचेरिनु उर आनंद न समात ।
निरखि निपट नैननि सुख तृण तोरत बलि
जात ॥
अति उदार बिबि सुन्दर सुरत सूर सुकुमार ।
जै श्री हित हरिवंश करौ दिन दोऊ अचल
बिहार ॥ ५८ ॥

तेरे हित लैन आई बन तैं श्याम पठाई,
हरति कामिनि घन कदन काम कौ ।
काहे कौं करत बाधा सुनिरि चतुर राधा,
भेटि कैं भेटि री माई प्रगट जगत मौ ॥

1. प्रिय

देखिरी रजनी नीकी रचना रुचिर पी की ,
पुलिन नलिन नभ उदित रोहिनी[1] धौ ।
तू तौव सखी सयानी तैं मेरी एकौ न मानी ,
हौं तोसौं कहत हारी जुवति जुगति[2] सौं ॥
मोहन लाल छबीलौ अपने रंग रंगीलौ ,
मोहत विहंग। पशु मधुर मुरली रौ ।
वे तौव गनत तन जीवन जोवन तव ,
जै श्री हित हरिवंश हरि भजहि भामिनि
जौ ॥ ५८ ॥

यह जु एक मन बहुत ठौर कहि कहि कौने
सचु पायौ ।
जहां तहां बिपति जार जुवती लौं प्रगट
पिंगला[3] गायौ ॥
द्वै तुरंग पर जोर चढत हठ परत कौन
पै धायौ ।

---

1 रोहिणी 2 युक्ति 3.(गणिका)
वेश्या

कहि धौं कौन अंक पर राखै जो गणिका[1]
सुत जायौ ॥
जै श्री हित हरिवंश प्रपंच बंच सब काल
व्याल[2] कौरवायौ ॥
यह जिय जानि श्याम श्यामा पद कमल
संगी सीर नायौ ॥५९॥

कहा कहौं इन नैंननि की बात,
ये अलि प्रिया बदन[3] अम्बुज रस अटके
अनत जन जात ॥
जब जब रुकत पलक सम्पुट लट अति
आतुर अकुलात ।
लंपट लव निमेष अन्तर तै अलप[4]
कलप सत सात ॥
श्रुतिपर कञ्ज दृगञ्जन कुच विच मृग
मद है न समात ।
जै श्री हित हरिवंश नाभि सर जलचर
जांचत सांवल गात
॥६०॥

1 गणिका 3 वदन
2 व्याल 4 अल्प कल्प

आजु सखी बन में जु बने प्रभु नाचत है
ब्रजमंडन
वैस[1] किशोर जुवति अंसनि पर दिये विमल
भुज दंडन ॥
कोमल कुटिल अलक सुठि सोभित[2]
अवलम्बित युग गंडन[3]।
मानहु मधुप थकित रस लम्पट नील
कमल के खंडन ॥
हास विलास हरत सबकौ मन काम
समूह विहंडन ।
जै श्री हित हरिवंश करत अपनौ
जस[4] प्रगट अखिल ब्रह्मंडन ॥
॥ ६२ ॥

---

1. वय:
2. शोभित
3. गंड
4. यश

खेलत रास दुलहिनी दूलहु ।
सुनहु न सखी सहित ललितादिक[1],
निरखि निरखि नैननि किन फूलहु ॥
अति कल मधुर महा मोहन धुनि[2],
उपजत हंससुता के कूलहू[3] ।
थेईथेई बचन मिथुन मुख निसरत,
सुनि सुनि देह दसा[4] किन भूलहु ॥
मृदु पदन्यास उठत कुंकुम रज[5],
अद्‌भुत बहत समीर दुकूलहु[6] ।
कबहुं स्याम स्यामा दसनांचल,
कच कुच हार छुवत भुज मूलहु ॥
अति लावन्य[7] रूप अभिनय गुन[8]
नाहिन कोटि काम समतूलहु ।

---

1. ललिता आदिक
2. ध्वनि
3. कूल
4. दशा
5. रजः
6. दुकूल
7 लावण्य
8. गुण

भ्रुकुटि विलास हास रस बरसत
जै श्री हित हरिवंश प्रेम रस झूलहु ॥

॥ ६२ ॥

मोहन मदन त्रिभंगी । मोहन मुनि मन रंगी।
मोहन मुनि सघन प्रगट परमानन्द[1] गुन
गम्भीर गुपाला[2]
सीस[3] किरीट श्रावण मणि कुण्डल उर[4] मंडित
बनमाला ।
पीताम्बर तन धातु[5] बिचित्रित कल
किंकिणि कटि चंगी ।
नख मणि तरणि[6] चरण सरसीरुह[7] मोहन
मदन त्रिभंगी
मोहन बेनु बजावै इहि रव नारि बुलावै ।
आई व्रज नारि सुनत वंशी स्वगृह पति
बधु बिसारे ।

---

1 परम आनन्द
2 गोपाल
3 शीर्ष
4 उर
5. देहवर्ण
6. सूर्य:
7. सरसीरुह

दरसन^1 मदन गोपाल मनोहर मनसिज ताप निवारे ।
हरषित वदन बंक अवलोकनि सरस मधुर धुनि गावै ।
मधुमय श्याम समान अधर धरि मोहन बेनु बजावै ॥
रास रच्यौ बन माहीं विमल कलप^2 तरु छाहीं ।
विमल कलप तरु तीर सुपेशाल सरद रैन बर चंदा^{3} ।
सीतल^4 मंद सुगंध पवन बहै तहां खेलत नंदनंदा ।
अदभुत^5 ताल मृदंग मनोहर किंकिनि शब्द कराहीं ।
यमुना पुलिन रसिक रस सागर रास रच्यौ बन माहीं ।

---

1. दर्शन 3. चन्द्रः 5. (अदभुत)
2. कल्पतरु 4. शीतल अद्भुत

देखत मधुकर केली मोहे खग मृग बेली
मोहे मृग धेनु सहित सुर सुन्दरि प्रेम
मगन पट छूटे ।
उडुगण चकित थकित शशि मण्डल
कोटि मदन मन लूटे ।
अधरपान परिरम्भन अतिरस आनंद
मगन सहेली
जै श्री हित हरिवंश रसिक सचु[1]
पावत देखत मधुकर केली ॥
॥ ६३ ॥

बेनु माई बाजै बंशी बट
सदा बसंत रहत वृन्दावन
पुलिन पवित्र सुभग यमुनातट ॥
जटित क्रीट[2] मकराकृत[3] कुण्डल,
मुख अरविंद भंवर मानों लट ।

1 सत्य 2 क्रीड 3 मकराकार

दसननि कुंद कली छवि लज्जित,
सज्जित कनक समान पीत पट ॥
मुनि मन ध्यान धरत नहिं पावत,
करत विनोद संग बालक भट[1] ।
दास अनन्य भजन रस कारन
जै श्री हित हरिवंश प्रगट लीला नट[2]
॥ ६४ ॥

मदन मथन धन निकुन्ज खेलत हरि,
राका रुचिर सरद रजनी ।
यमुना पुलिन तट सुर तरु के निकट,
रचित रास चलि मिलि सजनी ।
बाजत मृदु मृदंग नाचत सबै सुधंग,
तै न श्रावन सुन्यौ बेनु बजनी ।
जै श्री हित हरिवंश प्रभु राधिका रमन[3]
मोकों ।
भावै माई जगत भगत भजनी ॥ ६५ ॥

---

1 भट: 2. नटन   3 रमण

विहरत दोऊ प्रीतम कुञ्ज
अनुपम गौर श्याम तन सोभा बन बरसत
सुख पुञ्ज ॥
अद्भुत[1] खेत[2] महा मनमथ कौ दुंदुभि भूषन
राव[3] ।
जूझत सुभट परस्पर अंग अंग उपजत
कोटिक भाव ॥
भर संग्राम श्रमित अति अबला निद्रायत
कल नैन ।
पिय के अंक निसंक तंक तन आलस
जुत कृत सैन ॥
लालन मिस आतुर पिय परसत उरू[4] नाभि
उर जात[5] ।
उद्भुत[6] छटा विलोकि अवनि पर विथकित
वेपथ गात ॥

---

1. अद्भुत 3. रव: 5. उरज
2. क्षेत्र 4. ऊरू 6 अद्भुत

नागरि निरखि मदन विष व्यापत[1] दियो
सुधाधर धीर ।
सत्वर ऊठे महा मधु पीवत मिलत मीन
मिव नीर[2]
अबही मैं मुख मध्य विलोके बिंबाधर[3]
सु रसाल
जाग्रत ज्यों भ्रम भयौ परयौ मनसत
मनासिज कुल जाल
सकृदपि[4] मयि अधरामृतमुपनय[5] सुन्दरि
सहज सनेह[6] ।
तव पद पंकजकौ निज मन्दिर पालय
सहि मम देह ॥
प्रिया कहत कहु कहां हुते पिय नव
निकुञ्ज वर राज

---

1 व्याप्त
2. नीर:
3. बिंब अधर
4. सकृद् अपि
5. अधर अमृत
6. स्नेह

सुन्दर वचन रचन कत वितरत[1] रतिलम्पट
बिनु काज ॥
इतनों श्रवन सुनत मानिनि मुख अन्तर
रह्यौ न धीर
मतिकातर विरहज दुःख व्यापत बहुतर
स्वाँस समीर ॥
जै श्री हित हरिवंश भुजन आकर्षे
लै राखे उर मांझ
मिथुन मिलत जु कछुक सुख उपज्यौ
त्रुटि लवमिव[2] भई सांझ ॥
॥ ६६ ॥

रुचिर राजत वधू कानन किशोरी
सरस षोडश किये, तिलक मृगमद दिये,
मृगज लोचन उबटि अंग शिर खोरी
गंड पँडीर मंडित, चिकुर चन्द्रिका
मेदिनी कवरि[3] गूंथित सुरंग डोरी
श्रवन ताटंक कै चिबुक पर बिन्दु दै

1 वितरति 2. लव इव 3 कवरी

कसुंभि कंचुकि दुरे उरज फल कोरी ॥
वलय कंकन दोति नखनि जावक[1] जोति ।
उदर गुण रेख[2] पट नील करि थोरी
सुभग जघन स्थली क्वनित[3] किंकिनि भली ,
कोक संगीत रस सिंधु झक झोरी
विविधि लीला रचित रहसि हरिवंश हित
रसिक सिर मौर राधारवन जोरी ।
भृकुटि निर्जित मदन , मंद सस्मित वदन
किये रस विवस[4] घनश्याम पिय गोरी ॥ ६७ ॥

---

1 यावक

2. त्रिवलि

3. क्वणित

4. विवश

रास में रसिक मोहन बने भामिनी ।

सुभग पावन पुलिन, सरस सौरभ नलिन,

मत्त मधुकर निकर, सरद की जामिनी ॥

त्रिविध रोचक पवन, ताप दिनमनि[1] दवन,

तहां ठाड़ रवन संग सत कामिनी ।

ताल बीना[2] मृदंग, सरस नाचत सुधंग,

एकतैं एक संगीत की स्वामिनी ॥

राग-रागनि जमी, बिपिन बरसत अमी,

अधर बिंबनि रमी मुरलि अभिरामिनी ॥

लाग कट्टर उरप सप्त सुर[3] सौं सुलप,

लेत सुन्दर सुघर राधिका नामिनी ॥

तत्त थेइ-थेइ करत गतिव नूतन धरत,

पलटि डगमग ढरत मत्त गज गामिनी ।

धाइ नवरँग धरी उरसि राजत खरी,

जै श्री उभै कल हंस हरिवंश घन दामिनी ॥

॥ ६८ ॥

---

1. दिनमणि

2. वीणा

3. सप्तस्वर

मोहिनी मोहन रंगे प्रेम सुरंगे,
मत्त मुदित कल नाचत सुधंगे
सकल कला प्रबीन[1], कल्यान रागिनी लीन,
कहत न बनै माधुरी अंग अंगे ॥
तरनि[2] तनया तीर, त्रिविध सखी समीर,
मानौं मुनि व्रत धरयौ कपोती, कोकिला, कीर ।
नागरि-नवकिशोर मिथुन मनसि चोर,
सरस गावत दोऊ मंजुल मन्दर घोर ॥
कंकन किंकिनि धुनि, मुखर नूपुरनि सुनि,
जै श्रीहितहरिवंश रस बरसै नव तरुनि ॥
॥ ६९ ॥

आज सम्हारत नाहिन गोरी ।
फूली फिरत मत्त करनी ज्यौं सुरत समुद्र झकोरी ।

1. प्रवीण
2. तरणि

आलस बलित अरुन धूसर मधि प्रगट
करत दृग चोरी
पिय पर करुण अमी रस बरसत अधर
अरुनता थोरी
बांधत भृंग उरज[1] अम्बुज पर अलक
निबन्ध किसोरी ।
संगम किरचि किरचि कंचुकि बंद
सिथिल भई कटि डोरी
देत असीस निरखि जुवति जन जिनकै
प्रीति न थोरी
जै श्री हित हरिवंश विपिन भूतल
पर संतत अविचल जोरी ॥
॥ ६० ॥

श्याम संग राधिका रास मंडल बनी
बीच नंद लाल व्रज बाल चंपक वरन,
ज्यों व घन तडित बिच कनक मर्कत
मनी

---

1 कुच कमल

लेत गति मान तत्त थेई हस्तक भेद
सरिगमपधनि[1] ये सप्त सुर नंदिनी
नित्य रस पहिर पट नील प्रकटित
छवि
वदन जनु जलद में मकरकी चंदिनी ॥
राग रागिनी तान मान संगीत मत[2]
थकित राकेस नभ सरद की जामिनी
जै श्री हित हरिवंश प्रभु हंस कटि
केहरी
दूरि कृत मदनमद मत्त गज गामिनी ॥
॥ ७२ ॥

सुन्दर पुलिन सुभग सुखदायक
नव नव घन अनुराग परस्पर,
खेलत कुंवर नागरी नायक ॥
सीतल[3] हंस सुता रसवीचिनी[4]

---

1. स रि ग म प ध नि
2. संमत
3. शीतल
4. वीचि, तरङ्ग

परसि पवन सीकर[1] मृदु बरसत ।
वर मन्दार कमल चम्पक कुल
सौरभ सरस मिथुन मन हरसत[2] ।
सकल सुधंग विलास पराबधि
नाचत नवल मिले सुर गावत[3]
मृगज मयूर मराल भ्रमर पिक
अद्भुत कोटि मदन सिर नावत[4] ॥
निर्मित कुसुम सयन मधुपूरित
भाजन कनक निकुञ्ज विराजत
रजनीमुख सुख रासि[5] परस्पर
सुरत समर दोऊ दल साजत
विट कुल नृपति किशोरी कर धृत
बुधि बल नीबी[6] बन्धन मोचत
नेति नेति बचनामृत[7] बोलत

---

1 शीकर
2. हारी
3. गायति
4. नमत्
5. राशि
6. नीवी
7 वचन अमृत

प्रणय कोप प्रीतम नाहिं सोचत ॥
जै श्री हित हरिवंश रसिक ललितादिक[1]
लता भवन रंध्रानि[2] अवलोकत
अनुपम सुख भर भरित विवस असु
आनन्द वारि कण्ठ दृग रोकत ॥

॥६२॥

खंजन मीन मृगज मद मेटत कहा
कहौ नैनन की बातें
सुनि सुन्दरी कहां लौं सिखईं मोहन
बसी करन की घातें ।
बंक निसंक चपल अनियारे अरुन स्याम
सित रचे कहां तें ।
डरत न हरत परायौ सर्बस मृदु मिव
मादिक दृग पातें ।
नेकु प्रसन्न दृष्टि पूरन करि नाहिं
मोतन चितयौ प्रमदा तें

1. ललिता आदिक

2. रन्ध्र

जै श्री हित हरिवंश हंस कल गामिनि
भावै सों करहु प्रेमके नातें ॥
॥ ६३ ॥

काहेको मान बढ़ावत है ,
बालक मृग लोचनि ।
हौंव डरनि कछु कहि न सकत
इक बात सकोचनि ॥
मत्त मुरलि अन्तर तव गावत
जाग्रत सैन तवाकृति[1] सोचनि ।
जै श्री हित हरिवंश महा मोहन पिय
आतुर विट विरहज दुःखमोचनि ॥
॥ ६४ ॥

हौं जु कहति इक बात ,
सखी सुनि काहे कों डारत ॥
प्राण रवन सौं क्यौं न करत ,
आगस[2] बिनु आरत[3] ॥

---

1 तव आकृति 2 आग : 3. आरात्

पिय चितवत तव चन्द्र वदन तन
 तू अध मुख निज चरण निहारत
वे मृदु चिबुक प्रलोप प्रबोधत
 तू भामिनि कर सौं कर टारत
विवस अधीर बिरह[1] अति कातर
 सर औ औसर[2] कछु वै न विचारत।
जै श्री हित हरिवंश रहसि प्रीतम मिलि,
 तृषित नैन काहे न प्रतिपारत ॥

॥ ६५ ॥

नागरी निकुंज ऐन किसलय दल रचित
 सैन
कोक कला कुसल कुंवर अति उदार री
सुरत रंग अंग अंग हावभाव भृकुटि
 भंग
माधुरी तरंग मथत कोटि मार री ॥
मुखर नूपुरनि सुभाव किंकिनी विचित्र
 राव ।

---

1 विरह 2. अवसर

विरमि[1] विरमि नाथ वदत वर विहार री ।
लाडिली किसोर राज हंस हंसिनी समाज
सींचत हरिवंश नयन सुरत सार री ॥

॥ ७६ ॥

लटकत फिरति जुवति रस फूली
लता भवन में सरस सकल निशि
पिय संग सुरत हिंडोरे झूली
जद्यपि[2] अति अनुराग रसासव[3] पान
बिबस नाहित गाति भूली ।
आलस बलित नैन विगलित लट
उर पर कछुक कंचुकी खूली ॥
मरगजि माल सिथिल[4] कटि बंधन
चित्रित कज्जल पीक दुकूली
जै श्री हित हरिवंश मदन सर जर जर
विथकित श्याम सजीवन मूली ॥

॥ ७७ ॥

---

1 विराम
2. यद्यपि
3. रसामृत , आसव
4 शिथिल

सुधंग नाचत नवल किशोरी
थेई थेई कहत चहत प्रीतम दिसि
वदन चन्द्र मनों तृषित चकोरी
तान बंधान मानमें नागरि
देखत श्याम कहत हो हो री
जै श्री हित हरिवंश माधुरी अंग
अंग
बरबल लियौ मोहन चित चोरी ॥
॥ ६८ ॥

रहसि रहसि मोहन पिय के संग री
लड़ैती अतिरस लटकत
सरस सुधंग अंग में नागरी
थेई थेई कहत अवनि पद पटकत
कोक कला कुल जानि सिरोमनि[1]
अभिनय कुटिल भृकुटियनि मटकति
बिवस भये प्रीतम अलिलम्पट
निरखि करज नासापुट चटकत

1 शिरोमणि

गुन[1] गान रसिके राइ[2] चूडामणि ,
रिझवत पदिक हार पट झटकत ।
जै श्री हित हरिवंश निकट दासी जन ,
लोचन चषक रसासव[3] गटकत ॥७९॥

वल्लवी सुकनक वल्लरी[4] तमाल श्याम संग
लाहि रही अंग अंग मनोभिरामिनी[5]
वदन जोति[6] मनों मयंक अलक तिलक
छवि कलंक
छपति श्याम अंक मानौ जलद दामिनी॥
बिगत वास हेम खम्भ[7] मनों भुवंग बेनी
दंड ,
पिय[8] के कंठ प्रेम पुंज कुंज कामिनी ।
जै श्री हित हरिवंश नाथ साथ सुरत
आलसवंत
उरज कनक कलस राधिका सुनामिनी ॥८०॥

1. गुण
2. राज
3. रस आसव
4. सुवर्णलता
5. मनस अभिरामिनी
6. ज्योति
7. हेमस्तम्भ
8. प्रिय

वृषभानुनंदिनी मधुर कल गावै ।
विकट औघर तान चर्चरी ताल सौं,
नन्दनन्दन मनसि मोद उपजावै ।
प्रथम मज्जन चारु चीर कज्जल तिलक,
श्रवन कुंडल वदन चंद्रनि लजावै
सुभग नक मेसरी रतन[1] हाटक[2] जरी
अधर बंधूक दसन कुंद चमकावै
वलय कंकन चारु उरसि राजत हारु
कटिव[3] किंकिनि चरन नूपुर बजावै
हंस कल गामिनी मथत मद कामिनी,
नखनि मदयंतिका रंग रुचि द्यावै ॥
निर्त सागर रभस रहसि नागरि नवल
चन्द्र चाली विविध भेदनि जनावै ।
कोक विद्या विदित भाइ अभिनय निपुन,
भ्रूविलासनि मकरकेतन नचावै ॥
निबिड़[4] कानन भवन बाहु रंजित रवन

---

1. रत्न
2. स्वर्ण
3. कटि
4. निबिड

सरस आलाप सुख पुंज बरसावै ।
उभय संगम सिंधु सुरत पूषन बंधु,
द्रवत मकरंद हरिवंश अलि पावै ॥

॥ ८२ ॥

नागरता की रासि किसोरी ।
नव नागरकुल मौलि सांवरौ,
बरबस कियौ चितै मुख मोरी ।
रूपरुचिर अंग अंग माधुरी,
बिनु भूषन भूषित ब्रज गोरी ।
छिन्न छिन्न कुसल सुधंग अंग में,
कोक रभस रस सिंधु झकोरी ॥
चंचल रसिक मधुप मोहन मन,
राखे कनक कमल कुच कोरी ।
प्रीतम नैन जुगल खंजन खग
बांधे विविध निबंधन डोरी ॥
अवनी उदर नाभि सरसी[1] में,
मनौं कछुक मादिक मधु घोरी,

1. सरसि

जै श्री हित हरिवंश पिवत सुन्दर वर,
सींव सुदृढ निगमनि की तोरी ॥

॥ ८२ ॥

छांड़ि दै मानिनी मान मन धरिबौ ।
प्रणद सुन्दर सुघर प्राण वल्लभ नवल,
वचन आधीन सौं इतो कत करिबौ ॥
जपत हरि बिबस तव नाम प्रतिपद विमल,
मनसि तव ध्यानतें निमिस[1] नहिं टरिबौ ।
घटत पल पल सुभग सरद की जामिनी,
भामिनी सरस अनुराग दिसि ढरिबौ ॥
हौं जु कछु कहत निजु बात सुनि मान
सखि,
सुमुखि बिनु काज घन विरह दुःख
भरिबौ ।
मिलत हरिवंश हित कुंज किसलय
सयन,
करत कल केलि सुख सिंधु में तरिबौ
॥ ८३ ॥

---

१. क्षण

आजु व देखियत है हो प्यारी रंग भरी।
मो पैं न दुरत चोरी वृषभानु की किसोरी,
शिथिल कटि की डोरी नंद के लालन सौं
सुरत लरी ॥
मुतियन लर टूटी चिकुर चन्द्रिका छूटी,
रहसि रसिक लूटी गंडनि[1] पीक परी।
नैननि आलस बस अधर बिंब निरस
पुलक,
प्रेम परस जै श्री हित हरिवंश री राजत
खरी। ॥८४॥

---

1. गण्डे

Charles S. J. White received his Ph.D. from The University of Chicago. A specialist in Indian religions and in medieval Hindi poetry, he is presently an associate professor of philosophy and religion, and director of the Center for Asian Studies, at The American University, Washington, D. C.

Asian Studies at Hawaii

No. 1 *Bibliography of English Language Sources on Human Ecology, Eastern Malaysia and Brunei.* Compiled by Conrad P. Cotter with the assistance of Shiro Saito. September 1965. Two parts. (Available only from Paragon Book Gallery, New York.)

No. 2 *Economic Factors in Southeast Asian Social Change.* Edited by Robert Van Niel. May 1968. Out of print.

No. 3 *East Asian Occasional Papers (1).* Edited by Harry J. Lamley. May 1969.

No. 4 *East Asian Occasional Papers (2).* Edited by Harry J. Lamley. July 1970.

No. 5 *A Survey of Historical Source Materials in Java and Manila.* Robert Van Niel. February 1971.

No. 6 *Educational Theory in the People's Republic of China: The Report of Ch'ien Chung-Jui.* Translated by John N. Hawkins. May 1971. Out of print.

No. 7 *Hai Jui Dismissed from Office.* Wu Han. Translated by C. C. Huang. June 1972.

No. 8 *Aspects of Vietnamese History.* Edited by Walter F. Vella. March 1973.

No. 9 *Southeast Asian Literatures in Translation: A Preliminary Bibliography.* Philip N. Jenner. March 1973.

No.10 *Textiles of the Indonesian Archipelago.* Garrett and Bronwen Solyom. October 1973. Out of print.

No.11 *British Policy and the Nationalist Movement in Burma, 1917–1937.* Albert D. Moscotti. February 1974.

No.12 *Aspects of Bengali History and Society.* Edited by Rachel Van M. Baumer. December 1975.

No.13 *Nanyang Perspective: Chinese Students in Multiracial Singapore.* Andrew W. Lind. June 1974.

No.14 *Political Change in the Philippines: Studies of Local Politics preceding Martial Law.* Edited by Benedict J. Kerkvliet. November 1974.

No.15 *Essays on South India.* Edited by Burton Stein. February 1976.

No.16 *The* Caurāsī Pad *of Śrī Hit Harivaṁś.* Charles S. J. White. 1977.

No.17 *An American Teacher in Early Meiji Japan.* Edward R. Beauchamp. June 1976.

No.18 *Buddhist and Taoist Studies I.* Edited by Michael Saso. In press.

No.19 *Sumatran Contributions to the Development of Indonesian Literature, 1920–1942.* Alberta Joy Freidus. 1977.

Orders for Asian Studies at Hawaii publications should be directed to The University Press of Hawaii, 2840 Kolowalu Street, Honolulu, Hawaii 96822. Present standing orders will continue to be filled without special notification.